Not just a book about sex, gender and the Swedish Parliament, Lena Wängnerud confronts the contemporaneous challenges of political representation, women's interests, masculinized political parties, and feminist institutionalism. A simple but nonetheless elegant argument is made: gender sensitive parliaments are constituted by gender sensitive parties, themselves made up of gender sensitive individuals. Marshalling extensive and persuasive data, Wängnerud identifies the individuals (male and female), institutions (especially parties), and wider contexts conducive to a gender sensitive politics. Any gender equality effect of the presence of women in parliaments, including the Swedish one, is never simply about numbers. A politics of presence is not enough. Changes, she writes, 'do not just happen'. Politics and gender scholars would do well, then, to apply her politics of feminist awareness approach so as to better understand the complicated relationship between women's descriptive and substantive representation.

Sarah Childs, University of Bristol

This excellent book turns the usual, unanswerable question, 'Do women make a difference in politics', into empirically answerable questions of the conditions for gender-sensitive parliaments.

Drude Dahlerup, Stockholm University, Sweden

The Principles of Gender-Sensitive Parliaments

Gender serves as a lens that makes visible important issues in the field of representation: Whom do elected politicians represent? What is at stake in the parliamentary process? What do we know about the interplay between parliaments and the everyday lives of citizens? It is widely understood that women's presence in government matters but we need to understand more clearly the conditions under which it matters.

Using Sweden as a case study, a country where the number of women elected to the national parliament has steadily risen since the 1970s, Lena Wängnerud presents a novel approach on which characteristics inside a parliament help to translate physical representation into substantive representation for women. Using three guiding principles, (i) the implementation of equal opportunities for women and men to influence internal parliamentary working procedures; (ii) the creation of room for women's interests and concerns on the political agenda; and (iii) the production of gender-sensitive legislation, Wängnerud shows what the necessary conditions are for women's needs, interests and concerns to be adequately integrated into parliamentary processes.

The Principles of Gender-Sensitive Parliaments adds fuel to all these classical debates within the field of political representation and will bring to the attention of a wider audience why electing women matters.

Lena Wängnerud is Professor at the University of Gothenburg. Her research focuses on representative democracy, gender and corruption, gender and anxiety. She has published in the *Annual Review of Political Science, European Political Science Review, Politics & Gender, Governance, Party Politics*, and *Scandinavian Political Studies*.

Routledge Research in Gender and Politics

1. **The Women's Movement in Protest, Institutions and the Internet**
Australia in transnational perspective
Sarah Maddison and Marian Sawer

2. **The Politics of Gender Culture under State Socialism**
An expropriated voice
Hana Havelková and Libora Oates-Indruchova

3. **Maternal Transition**
A North-South politics of pregnancy and childbirth
Candace Johnson

4. **The Principles of Gender-Sensitive Parliaments**
Lena Wängnerud

The Principles of Gender-Sensitive Parliaments

Lena Wängnerud

NEW YORK AND LONDON

First published 2015
by Routledge
711 Third Avenue, New York, NY 10017

and by Routledge
2 Park Square, Milton Park, Abingdon, Oxon OX14 4RN

Routledge is an imprint of the Taylor & Francis Group, an informa business

© 2015 Taylor & Francis

The right of Lena Wängnerud to be identified as author of this work has been asserted by her in accordance with sections 77 and 78 of the Copyright, Designs and Patents Act 1988.

All rights reserved. No part of this book may be reprinted or reproduced or utilised in any form or by any electronic, mechanical, or other means, now known or hereafter invented, including photocopying and recording, or in any information storage or retrieval system, without permission in writing from the publishers.

Trademark notice: Product or corporate names may be trademarks or registered trademarks, and are used only for identification and explanation without intent to infringe.

British Library Cataloguing in Publication Data
A catalogue record for this title has been requested

Library of Congress Cataloging in Publication Data
Wängnerud, Lena.
The principles of gender-sensitive parliaments / Lena Wängnerud.
   pages cm
Includes bibliographical references and index.
   1. Women legislators. 2. Legislative bodies. I. Title.
   HQ1236.W365 2015
   328.082–dc23
         2014042146

ISBN: 978-1-138-80265-0 (hbk)
ISBN: 978-1-315-75408-6 (ebk)

Typeset in Sabon
by Taylor & Francis Books

Contents

List of illustrations		x
List of abbreviations		xi
Preface		xii
1	Introduction	1
2	Gender-sensitive political parties	18
3	Gender-sensitive political representatives	36
4	Internal parliamentary working procedures	59
5	Room for women's interests and concerns	82
6	The production of gender-sensitive legislation	104
7	The politics of feminist awareness	131
	Appendix I: a note on the methodology	145
	Appendix II: a note on Swedish politics	150
	Index	156

Illustrations

Figures

1.1	Distinguishing between numbers of women elected and gender sensitivity	5
2.1	Number of women in the Swedish parliament, 1971–2014 (%)	22
2.2	Subjective left–right self-placement by Swedish MPs, 1985–2010	25
2.3	Attitudes among Swedish MPs toward two arguments for an equal distribution of women and men in the parliament, 1994–2010 (% "very important")	28
2.4	Attitudes toward two arguments for an equal distribution of women and men in parliament among MPs in center-right political parties, 1994–2010 (% "very important")	31
2.5	Comparing Swedish and Danish MPs: attitudes toward two different arguments for an equal distribution of women and men, 1994 and 2010 (% "very important")	32
3.1	Political interest among women and men in Sweden, 1960–2010 (% of very and fairly interested)	42
3.2	Proportion of voters in Sweden who support specific proposals, 1985–2010 (%)	46
3.3	Proportion of Swedish MPs who answered that it was "very important" to promote women's interests and concerns, 1985–2010 (%)	50
3.4	The development of newly elected MPs' commitment to women's issues and concerns over four terms (%)	53
4.1	Percentage of standing committees in the Swedish parliament with a woman in the presidency, 1985–2014	63
4.2	Proportion of women in social welfare committees compared with economy/technology committees, 1971–2014	66
5.1	Proportion of Swedish MPs who have gender equality as an area of personal interest, 1985–2010 (%)	87
5.2	Proportion of Swedish MPs who have welfare politics as an area of personal interest, 1985–2010 (%)	92

5.3	Proportion of Swedish MPs and voters who support specific proposals, 1985–2010 (%)	95
5.4	Gender equality and welfare politics as areas of personal interest and attitudes toward the proposals to ban all forms of pornography and introduce a six-hour workday among MPs considered strong versus weak feminists, 1985, 1994, and 2010 (%)	98
5.5	Acting in the interests of women	99
6.1	Percentage of women on municipal councils in Sweden, 1973–2010	115
7.1	Feminist awareness as a driving force toward a gender-sensitive parliament	134
7.2	Situating the contemporary Swedish Riksdag in the tension between a high number of women elected and gender sensitivity	135
7.3	Acting in the interests of women, workers, and immigrants	141

Tables

2.1	The number of women in parliamentary party groups in Sweden, 1985–2014 (%)	24
2.2	Determinants of attitudes among Swedish MPs toward two arguments for an equal distribution of women and men in parliament, 1994 and 2010 (logistic regression)	30
3.1	The three most important policy areas in Swedish voters' choice of party, 1985–2010	44
3.2	Determinants of Swedish MPs' commitment to represent women's issues and concerns 1988, 1994, and 2010 (logistic regression)	51
3.3	Self-defined champions of women's interests and how they perceive the argument that there will be consequences for policies (%)	55
4.1	Proportion of women on standing committees, 1971–2014	65
4.2	Swedish MPs' assessments of their personal contact with cabinet ministers, government officials, and party organizations, 1985–2010 (% reporting contact at least once a week)	68
4.3	Swedish MPs' assessments of working conditions, 1988, 2006, and 2010 (% satisfied)	70
4.4	Determinants of Swedish MPs' assessments of party group working conditions, 1988, 2006, and 2010 (logistic regression)	71
4.4.1	Proportion satisfied with their own party group working conditions in 2010	72
4.5	Swedish MPs' assessments of their ability to impact their own party groups' positions (%)	73

x   List of illustrations

4.6	Determinants of Swedish MPs' assessments of their ability to impact their own party groups' positions, 1988, 2006, and 2010 (logistic regression)	74
4.6.1	Proportion answering "very good" to the question about MPs' ability to make an impact on their own party groups in 2010	75
5.1	Swedish MPs' assessment of their personal contact with women's organizations, 1985–2010 (%)	86
5.2	The top three policy areas among women and men MPs and voters, 1985–2010	91
5.3	Determinants of Swedish MPs' priorities for welfare politics as an area of personal interest, 2002, 2006, and 2010 (logistic regression)	93
6.1	Official definition and national coordination of gender equality in Sweden	107
6.2	Gender-sensitive legislation, 1842–1970	109
6.3	Gender-sensitive legislation, 1971–2011	111
6.4	The effect of female councilors in Swedish municipalities, 1985–2006, on women's income, full-time employment, and parental leave in relation to men's (OLS regression, unstandardized b-coefficients, standard errors in parentheses)	118
6.5	Top countries in gender-equality rankings from Social Watch and World Economic Forum, 2007 and 2012/13	122
6.6	Explanations for variation in gender equality in the everyday lives of citizens, a worldwide comparison (OLS stepwise multivariate regression, coefficients, and adjusted R^2 included)	124
A.1	Number of survey respondents (women/men)	147
A2a	The gender gap in party choice in Sweden, 1956–2010	154
A2b	The gender gap in party choice in Sweden, 1956–2010	155

Abbreviations

Cen	Center Party
CEO	chief executive officer
ChrDem	Christian Democratic Party
Con	Conservative Party
diff.	difference
EU	European Union
GDI	Gender-related Development Index
GDP	gross domestic product
GEM	Gender Empowerment Index
Grn	Green Party
Lft	Left Party
Lib	Liberal Party
Ln	natural logarithm
MP	member of parliament
n.a.	not applicable (party not represented in parliament)
NewDem	New Democracy Party
NGO	nongovernmental organization
OECD	Organisation for Economic Co-operation and Development
OLS	ordinary least squares
RNGS	Research Network on Gender, Politics and the State
SE	standard error
sig.	significance
SNES	Swedish National Elections Study Program
SocDem	Social Democratic Party
SweDem	Sweden Democrats
UN	United Nations

Preface

I started work on this book when I was Visiting Research Scholar at the University of California, Berkeley, in 2009/10. I gained tremendously from attending the seminars, but most important, perhaps, were the frequent walks with a cup of coffee up to the top terrace. Standing there, I had a view over the Bay Area and the Golden Gate Bridge. This is the kind of environment that encourages big thoughts. Back at the University of Gothenburg I got stuck in to everyday life of academia – giving lectures, doing administrative work, writing papers and articles instead of a book. One morning, however, I woke up determined that I should finish the book on which I had started work, and here it is.

When I finally picked up the manuscript I realized that I had learned a lot from all the work that seemed like "bits and pieces" and I would like thank all the people I have collaborated with in recent years: Stefan Dahlberg, Carl Dahlström, Monika Djerf-Pierre, Peter Esaiasson, Mikael Gilljam, Marcia Grimes, Sören Holmberg, Anna Högmark, Bengt Johansson, Andrej Kokkonen, Staffan Kumlin, Elin Naurin, Henrik Ekengren Oscarsson, Maria Oskarson, Bo Rothstein, Helena Stensöta, Anders Sundell, Aksel Sundström, Rickard Svensson, Marcus Samanni, and Patrik Öhberg. We have worked together on papers, articles, and book chapters and I'm happy for all the good discussions! I know that Gothenburg is not Berkeley – I miss the view from the top terrace – but the research environment in Gothenburg is vibrant and, not least important, supportive. Big thoughts get criticized but always with the intention to make things better. A special thanks to Anna Högmark, who helped me with the statistical analyses.

I am grateful for the funding from The Swedish Foundation for Humanities and Social Sciences and The Swedish Research Council for Health, Working Life and Welfare, which made my visit to Berkeley possible, and also for other forms of funding that have supported my research. I am also grateful for the invitation I had from the Charles and Louise Travers Department of Political Science at UC Berkeley, and especially to Laura Stoker who helped me to organize the visit.

I want to dedicate this book to Sara, Sofie, Dejonte and Araceli. The four of you met at Oxford Elementary School in Berkeley and become friends. After a year, Sara and Sofie moved back to Sweden but I believe that the diversity at Oxford Elementary School had a long-lasting impact. You come from different backgrounds and you enriched each other's lives. I hope this book will enrich the lives of many readers and perhaps one day, when the four of you grow up, it will reach your hands too. At least, I have had you in mind while working on this book.

Why did I want to write this book? The fact that gender matters in politics fascinates me. I was brought up to feel that it should not matter. I wanted to contribute knowledge on how structures such as gender affect our lives and how we, at the same time, are able to change our life circumstances.

Lena Wängnerud
Gothenburg, March 2015

1 Introduction

> At the Social Democratic Party Congress, Mr. Palme held one of his many visionary speeches. This time on equality for women. It is excellent. We all rejoice in the topic selection. But pretty speeches to women are nothing new, Mr. Palme! Women have been listening to many of those over the years. Speeches must be followed by action – otherwise there will be no equality or freedom of choice.
> (Gunnar Helén, at the Liberal Party Congress, Sweden, November 25, 1972)

It is November 25, 1972. The leader of the Liberal Party in Sweden, Gunnar Helén, enters the scene. In front of him are members of his own party; however, it is obvious that he has a wider audience in mind. Helén is attacking the leader of the Social Democratic Party, Olof Palme. In September 1972 the Social Democratic Party had held its national congress, and the fact that Palme had devoted almost all of his speech to gender equality had attracted a great deal of attention. Now, Helén wanted to show that his party should also be taken seriously. Helén criticized Palme for his lack of concrete proposals, and he ended his speech at the Liberal Party Congress with the promise that internal boards of the Liberal Party would aim for an even distribution of women and men, with no less than 40 percent of either sex.[1] This was the first time in Sweden that a specific proportion, 40 percent, had been identified as a target for women's representation (Freidenvall 2006; Wängnerud 2001).

In 1972 a long journey started in Sweden. An election was held the following year, and the number of women in the Swedish parliament, the Riksdag, increased from 14 to 21 percent. This was a remarkable achievement. Since then, there has been only one occasion with a corresponding increase, seven percentage points, and that was the 1994 election, when the proportion of women in the Swedish Riksdag increased from 34 to 41 percent (Bergqvist et al. 2000).

What characterizes both the 1973 and 1994 elections is that issues of gender equality were high on the political agenda. More important to note, however, is that the major political parties promised to deliver visible changes. In 1973 the promises were about changes to internal party boards, and in 1994 they were about external party lists. These examples illustrate this book's main point: *changes do not just happen*. To understand changes in gender equality, we need to analyze actors geared toward changing the status of women vis-à-vis men. We also need a benchmark against which actions can be evaluated; not all actions lead to success. This is the second major point of the book: there is *no linear process* leading to gender equality. The journey that started in Sweden in 1972 has not been easy, and it is by no means over.

Sweden is, by most standards, considered one of the most gender-equal countries in the world. From the Swedish case we can learn about the role that parliaments, or legislatures more broadly, play in transforming society.[2] More specifically, we can learn under what circumstances parliaments can play a role. As stated previously, changes do not just happen. In representative democracies, political parties are key actors, and parliaments do not change unless major political parties want them to (Dahlerup and Leyenaar 2013; Kittilson 2006; Osborn 2012). Moreover, political parties do not change automatically. In this book, we shall look at exogenous factors – external shocks – affecting parties, but even more energy will be devoted to endogenous factors, such as an effect of individuals within parties. Thus, there are three levels of analysis: the level of parliaments as institutions, the level of political parties, and the level of individual politicians. The argument is that gender-sensitive parliaments are made up of gender-sensitive political parties, which in turn are made up of gender-sensitive politicians. In this way a gender-sensitive parliament becomes a non-static phenomenon; the exact nature of a gender-sensitive parliament varies across time and across countries.

Why study parliaments?

The question arises: Why study parliaments? One way to answer this question is to look at transformations of citizens' everyday lives one country at a time. Over the past four decades Sweden has experienced major changes in spheres of society related to gender equality: In 1970 about 10 percent of children in Sweden aged one to six years were registered in day care; in 2009 the corresponding figure was 90 percent (the vast majority in municipal day care). In 1974 men in Sweden gained the right to parental leave on the same terms as women. The statistics tell us that in the 1970s no days (i.e. 0 percent of days) for which parental allowance was paid were claimed by men, but in 2009 the corresponding figure was above 20 percent. During the same period women's participation in higher education and in the paid labor force increased strongly in Sweden.[3]

Another way to answer the question "Why study parliaments?" is to highlight variations across countries. Several international organizations produce measurements of gender equality. In 2012 Sweden was ranked among the top countries in the Save the Children mothers' index, which captures the situation of mothers and small children. Countries such as the United States and Japan were ranked lower on the list. Rankings produced by Social Watch and the World Economic Forum similarly placed Sweden among the top countries, ranking the United States and Japan considerably lower. Social Watch and the World Economic Forum focus on gender gaps in areas such as educational attainment, economic participation and opportunity, health and survival, and empowerment.[4] It is interesting to note that Sweden has a high number of female legislators, currently 44 percent in the Riksdag. The corresponding figure for the United States is 18 percent women in the House of Representatives, and for Japan, 8 percent women in the Shugiin, the Japanese House of Representatives (www.ipu.org).

The results presented above refer to three of the most economically developed countries in the world. Thus, we can conclude that gender equality is not determined by economic development or modernization alone (cf. Inglehart and Norris 2003). It would be reasonable to believe that political institutions such as parliaments matter, and more precisely that it is the composition of these institutions that is important, but this assumption cannot be taken for granted. The idea of this book is to provide new tools to study the role of parliaments in processes related to gender equality. This ambition includes development of theory as well as empirical investigation.

The argument

The argument, stated previously, is that gender-sensitive parliaments are made up of gender-sensitive political parties, which in turn are made up of gender-sensitive politicians. In this way a gender-sensitive parliament becomes a non-static phenomenon; the exact nature of a gender-sensitive parliament varies across time and across countries. The first step of this book is to present a tentative model of a gender-sensitive parliament. In this way we get a benchmark against which actions by political parties and individual politicians can be evaluated.

Distinguishing between numbers of women elected and gender sensitivity

The ideas presented in this book should be seen as a development of the ideas presented by Anne Phillips (1995) in her influential book *The Politics of Presence*. Phillips (1991, 1995, 2007) argues that societies will not achieve equality between women and men simply by disregarding gender-related differences. She contends that women's interests and concerns will be inadequately addressed in a politics dominated by men:

> There are particular needs, interests, and concerns that arise from women's experience, and these will be inadequately addressed in a politics dominated by men. Equal rights to a vote have not proved strong

enough to deal with this problem; there must also be equality among those elected to office.

(Phillips 1995, 66)

Numerous empirical studies show that women politicians all over the world tend to be more active than their male colleagues when it comes to placing equality policy on the political agenda.[5] The conclusion from Scandinavian countries, where the number of women elected has been high for quite some time, is that there has been a shift in emphasis as the number of women in parliament has increased, with women's interests being accorded greater scope and a more prominent place on the political agenda (Bergqvist et al. 2000; Skjeie 1992; Wängnerud 2000). However, the closer one gets to outcomes in the everyday lives of citizens, the fewer empirical findings there are to report. A typical conclusion from research on outcomes is that effects of having a high number of women elected are smaller than anticipated in theory (Bratton and Ray 2002; Schwindt-Bayer and Mishler 2005; Wängnerud and Sundell 2012).

Scholars in the field distinguish between *descriptive representation*, the number of women elected to parliaments, and *substantive representation*, effects of women's presence in parliaments (Celis and Childs 2008; Krook and Childs 2010; Wängnerud 2009). The theory of the politics of presence gives reason to expect a link between descriptive and substantive representation. Phillips's line of reasoning represents mainstream argumentation in research on women in politics:

Women have distinct interests in relation to child-bearing (for any foreseeable future, an exclusively female affair); and as society is currently constituted they also have particular interests arising from their exposure to sexual harassment and violence, their unequal position in the division of paid and unpaid labor and their exclusion from most arenas of economic or political power.

(Phillips 1995, 67–68)

Women politicians are expected to be better representatives of women's interests and concerns, since they, at least to some extent, share experiences with women voters. However, based on her studies in the United States, Deborah Dodson (2006, 8) writes about a relationship between descriptive and substantive representation that is probabilistic rather than deterministic. Along the same lines, Karen Celis and Sarah Childs (2008, 419) state that the argument is simple: Women, when present in politics, are more likely to act for women than men are. However, the conclusion is complex; there is no guarantee that they will actually do so.

Phillips (1995, 188) uses the metaphor "a shot in the dark" to mitigate high expectations. Her doubts stem from knowledge about rigid institutions; parliaments do not change easily. Joni Lovenduski (2005, 48), a distinguished scholar of British politics, argues that the most difficult obstacle that female politicians meet is the deeply embedded culture of masculinity in political institutions. She recognizes hindrances to women politicians, such as hostile reactions to women, working conditions that are incompatible with family responsibilities, and the existence of male-dominated networks.

I want to push this research further by recognizing the distinction between numbers of women elected and gender sensitivity. The fundamental research question is the same in this book as in *The Politics of Presence* (and a plethora of other studies): *What are the necessary conditions for women's interests and concerns to be adequately integrated into political processes?* I take as my point of departure the insight that the mere presence of women politicians is not enough – that is, that the relationship between descriptive and substantive representation is probabilistic rather than deterministic, and I present tools for analyzing this relationship.

Figure 1.1 visualizes the separation of the dimensions "number of women elected" and "gender sensitivity." The theory of the politics of presence predicts that when the proportion of women increases, the political process will work better in terms of integrating women's interests and concerns. In Figure 1.1 this idea is represented by Country A. However, it may be the case that gender-sensitive *political parties* compensate for the lack of women politicians, for example, through a feminist party leader or strong connections with non-parliamentary women's organizations. Then we could end up with the

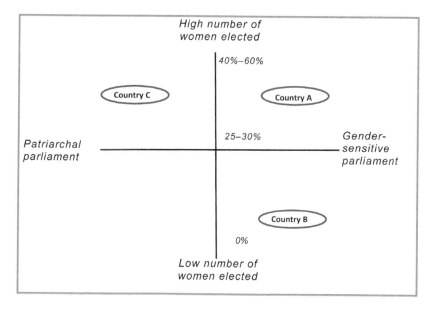

Figure 1.1 Distinguishing between numbers of women elected and gender sensitivity

same result as Country A in terms of gender sensitivity, but with other mechanisms at work. In Figure 1.1 this idea is represented by Country B.

A third alternative to reflect on is that obstacles to women politicians are so severe that despite their presence in higher proportions, few visible changes are taking place. This is Country C in Figure 1.1. A Country D (not included in Figure 1.1), representing the ultimate patriarchal situation is, of course, a fourth potential alternative. This book, however, focuses on modernized countries considered free, according to established measures of democracy, and alternative D thereby becomes less interesting. It becomes more relevant if one thinks of the model in Figure 1.1 as a tool for comparing political parties, not entire parliaments. There are, for example, good reasons to expect radical right parties to be found in the lower left corner of the model. Empirical research shows that radical right-wing parties tend to be heavily male dominated in terms of personnel as well as ideas (Norris 2005).

At this stage, the model in Figure 1.1 is a tentative one. A more elaborate model will be presented in the last chapter of the book. The intention is to develop a theory of gender-sensitive parliaments that works for comparisons across time, across countries, and also across political parties within countries.

Before moving on, we need a definition of gender sensitivity. What are the endpoints on the horizontal axis in Figure 1.1? This introductory chapter discusses only gender-sensitive parliaments. Political parties and individual politicians will be addressed in subsequent chapters.

A preliminary definition of a gender-sensitive parliament

I believe that we need new tools for studying women in politics. The number of studies in the field is growing and analyses are becoming increasingly sophisticated. Still, there is a lack of research in which scholars try to put pieces of information together. In order to give a credible answer to the research question, *What are the necessary conditions for women's interests and concerns to be adequately integrated into political processes?* we need several pieces of information. First, do women entering politics meet gender-specific obstacles and, if so, how great are those obstacles? Second, we need information on who, if anyone, is creating room for women's interests and concerns on the political agenda. Finally, we need information on success: Do parliaments produce gender-sensitive legislation? One cannot judge the quality of the political processes on sole indicators.[6] Representative democracies are complex systems, and in order to understand the role of parliaments correctly we need information from a multitude of sources. This does not mean that everything is equally interesting. In this book, I square the circle in the following three parts.

Internal parliamentary working procedures

The concept of "critical mass" is intensely debated in scholarship on women in politics. Some scholars seek to identify a threshold number or a tipping point at which the impact of women's presence in parliament becomes apparent; a figure of around 30 percent is often mentioned. Others criticize the concept of critical mass as being too mechanical and implying immediate change at a certain level. They focus instead on "critical acts" (Dahlerup 1988) to explore two questions: Who is pushing for change consistent with women's interests, and what kinds of strategies are useful (Dahlerup 2006a)? Still others (e.g. Grey 2006) suggest that different thresholds have to be recognized in studies on women in parliament; for example, attaining a proportion of 15 percent may allow women politicians to change the political agenda, but 40 percent may be needed for women-friendly policies to be introduced.

The question of how the presence of women affects behavior and culture within political institutions is multilayered. The question is not just about whether women politicians behave differently, or whether they meet certain obstacles, or whether, beyond a certain threshold of numbers, they are able to make an impact. The question also concerns whether their presence has an impact on the behavior of men, either reinforcing gender differences or modifying them. For example, one area of contention is how to interpret functional divisions between women and men; that is, the existence of gender patterns related to areas of responsibility, such as women politicians being well represented in committees dealing with gender-equality or social welfare issues but not in committees dealing with foreign affairs or financial issues. Is the existence of such patterns a hindrance or not? Analyses of parliamentary internal working procedures also need to cover information on formal power positions from a gender perspective, and how male and female politicians themselves perceive their ability to make an impact.

Room for women's interests and concerns

What do women do in parliaments? In most Western democracies, it is possible to find examples of prominent women politicians in areas such as foreign affairs and finance, as well as in education or family policy. However, the core issue in research on substantive representation does not concern "what women do in parliaments" but, more specifically, the extent to which the number of women elected affects women's interests. Phillips (1995, 47) argues that gender equality among those elected to office is desirable because of the changes it can bring about: "It is representation ... with a purpose, it aims to subvert or add or transform." This corresponds with Hanna Pitkin's (1967, 209) classical definition of political representation: "Representation here means acting in the interest of the represented, in a manner responsive to them." For interests to get attention, someone needs to act.

Empirical research shows that not all women politicians are active in the area of gender equality. Moreover, it is obvious that some male politicians are active in this field. Anne Phillips states that there *must* be equality among those elected to office. A slightly different approach is found in the writings of

Iris Marion Young. What is highlighted in Young's alternative approach is the importance of group awareness. Instead of focusing on the experiences shared by women politicians and women voters, the group awareness approach concentrates on the formulation and implementation of programs explicitly aimed at transforming society. It is important to note that the theory of group awareness does not ascribe importance to women politicians per se, but to politicians who are sensitive to social group experiences. The emphasis in the following quotation from Young is on giving voice and expressing experiences:

> First, I feel represented when someone is looking after the interests I take as mine and share with some others. Secondly, it is important to me that the principles, values, and priorities that I think should guide political decisions are voiced in discussion. Finally, I feel represented when at least some of those discussing and voting on policies understand and express the kind of social experience I have because of my social group position and the history of social group relations.
> (Young 2000, 134)

My interpretation is that in the theory of group awareness, *intentionality* is a core mechanism; in order to represent women – or any other disadvantaged group in society – politicians must be explicitly aware of the social position of that group.

In sum, analyses of the room given to women's interests and concerns need, first of all, to identify what these interests and concerns are. Then the next step is to try to capture their scope and prominence on an institutional, collective level. It is only when we try to get at the mechanisms at work that we need to ask questions about the effects of social background characteristics (as suggested by Phillips) and the intentional representation of social groups (as suggested by Young).

The production of gender-sensitive legislation

This book focuses on formal political institutions. However, what is at stake is the real-world problem of large variations in women's lives across time and across countries. In a recent study Mala Htun and Laurel Weldon (2012) cover developments in 70 countries over four decades. They set out to explain policy changes in the area of violence against women, and they demonstrate that feminist mobilization in civil society is the critical factor accounting for changes in women-friendly directions.

In another recent study, Eunhye Yoo (2012) analyzes changes in governments' recognition of women's rights in 134 countries during the period 1984–2003. In accordance with Htun and Weldon's study, Yoo demonstrates that feminist mobilization, here concretized in relation to women's international nongovernmental organizations, has an effect, but the effect is restricted to the area of women's political rights. The effect of women's international non-governmental organizations is not evident in the analyses of women's economic or social rights (ibid., 2012, 331).

The above-mentioned studies are important, since they focus on essential dimensions of women's lives and conduct credible tests including a large number of control variables. Both studies question the impact of women's presence in formal political institutions. In essence, the question is, does the presence of women in parliaments have an effect? At this stage, my answer is that to analyze such issues we need new and better tools than research has provided so far. Legislation and policies, areas highlighted by Htun and Weldon (2012) and Yoo (2012), however, need to be taken into account in the creation of such tools.

I suggest that a fully gender-sensitive parliament is one where women and men have equal opportunity to influence internal parliamentary working procedures, where there is generous room for women's interests and concerns on the political agenda, and where gender-sensitive legislation is produced in a satisfactory way. The opposite of a gender-sensitive parliament would be a fully patriarchal parliament, one where women are systematically discriminated against, where there is no room for women's interests and concerns on the political agenda, and where legislation reproduces gender-based power structures over and over again. This reasoning is in line with the definitions of "male dominance" versus "gender balance" in politics, provided by Drude Dahlerup and Monique Leyenaar (2013, 8, 232). In their models, however, the number of women elected is presented as one dimension among several others – that is, as part of a package measuring male dominance/gender balance. My study is different, as I raise the question of *to what extent* the number of women elected is a driving force behind a gender-sensitive, non-patriarchal parliament.

Development of theory will be an ongoing activity throughout the book. This means refining concepts, models, and the selection of indicators to arrive at well-founded principles of a gender-sensitive parliament. This ambition includes thinking carefully about whether the suggested areas work in tandem, or if we get different results depending on whether the area studied is internal working procedures, room for women's interests and concerns, or production of gender-sensitive legislation.

The debate on self-authorization

In the mid-1990s an influential Research Network on Gender, Politics and the State (RNGS) was established. Dorothy E. McBride and Amy G. Mazur, two leading scholars, write that research in the network is necessarily about representation:

> The core question of the work ... is whether, how, and why women's policy agencies have been effective partners for women's movements

and their actors in gaining access to state policy-making arenas and influencing policy outcomes. Bringing women's movements into the state is necessarily about representation; therefore, this study on state feminism is ultimately about the process of making democracies more democratic.

(ibid., 2010, 3)

The RNGS is founded on a state feminism framework. McBride and Mazur (2010, 4) remind us that Helga Hernes (1987) coined the term and that the original aim was to give a name to the idea that governments could pursue feminist aims and promote women-friendly policies. Gradually, the term "state feminism" has come to include a package of ideas and structures; terms such as "women's policy machinery," "gender-equality offices," and "women's rights agencies" are used to identify those branches within the state that are responsible for preparing decision making and implementing policies in the field of gender equality.

The RNGS is part of a burgeoning field of research where *self-authorization* is upgraded, and authorization through general elections devalued, as key components in democratic processes. In the citation above, McBride and Mazur state that bringing women's movements into the state is "necessarily about representation" and "making democracies more democratic." They make the women's movement, not women citizens, into the most important reference point in studies on representation.

In his book *The Representative Claim*, Michael Saward (2010) brings forward a line of reasoning similar to that found within the RNGS. Saward argues for a theory in which political representation is seen as a "dynamic process of claim-making and not ... as a static fact of electoral politics" (ibid., 3). In this strand of research, claim-making processes are seen as the important drivers of political change. Informal institutions and self-authorized representatives are regarded as equal to formal institutions and representatives authorized through general elections. In fact, Saward rejects the use of "binary thinking" that distinguishes, for example, between self-authorization and authorization through elections (ibid., 41).

The aim of this burgeoning field of research is to reveal more inclusive ways of understanding politics. However, it is controversial, indeed, to blur distinctions between different types of representation. The question of *accountability* has been raised by some scholars within the RNGS. Joni Lovenduski and Marika Guadagnini (2010, 173) state that the RNGS assumes that movement actors speak for women as a group. They are critical of this assumption, however, and make the point that accountability needs to be contextualized:

> At the system level, accountability is a function of the institution in which representatives act. So, where movement actors are in the legislatures they are accountable to their electorate, their parties, and their

constituencies. Where movement actors are in trade unions, they are accountable to their members and co-workers, whereas in parties they are answerable to their fellow members but also more indirectly to the electorate and to the interests that are the basis of party support.

(ibid., 2010, 186)

Lovenduski and Guadagnini raise the important question of who has the mandate to speak for whom. They go so far as to characterize accountability as the "hidden dragon" of women and politics research (Lovenduski and Guadagnini 2010, 191). I agree that we need to recognize that it is actors within parliaments/legislatures who have the mandate to speak for "their electorate, their parties, and their constituencies," which are comparatively broad layers of the population. To me, what makes a fundamental difference is that a general election, even with its shortcomings, is an outstanding control station in democratic processes. This goes back to Pitkin's classic definition of political representation, cited previously: "Representation here means acting in the interest of the represented, in a manner responsive to them." The ballot makes it possible to check levels of support among broad layers of the population. Self-authorized actors come without codified control stations, and thus they are risky comrades; how can we know if women's movements are responsive to women citizens? In the end, it is citizens and not movements that are the funding actors in democratic states.

The ambition of this book is to find a way to combine dynamic understandings of politics with formal institutions. However, the important lesson to be learned from research inspired by "claim making" and "women's policy machinery" is that to judge the quality of the parliamentary process, we need reference points outside the parliament itself. Moreover, this strand of research reminds us that the *political process* is a wider phenomenon than the *parliamentary process*. Societies do change. However, we know all too little about the role parliaments play in such transformations. In this sense, the focus in this book on gender equality and the Swedish case serves as a lens for studying classic issues in the field of political representation: Whom do elected politicians represent? What is at stake in the parliamentary process? What do we know about the interplay between parliaments and the everyday lives of citizens?

The choice to study Sweden

This book takes presence theories one step further. Sweden is a country where the number of women elected to the national parliament has been high for quite some time. During the 1970s Sweden crossed the threshold of 20 percent women in parliament; the proportion climbed past 30 percent during the 1980s, and 40 percent during the 1990s. Currently, women hold 44 percent of the seats in Sweden's parliament; the average for national parliaments in Europe is 25.3 percent (the worldwide average is 22.2

percent).[7] Sweden can therefore be seen as a useful laboratory in which to study the complicated relationship between descriptive and substantive representation.

Another reason for studying Sweden is that it is a country for which there exists an impressive amount of data. The data that will be used in this book consist of statistics from official records, but most important will be the use of a unique set of surveys of Swedish members of parliament conducted by scholars at the Department of Political Science at the University of Gothenburg. The Swedish Parliamentary Surveys were conducted in 1985, 1988, 1994, 1998, 2002, 2006, and 2010 (lowest response rate 89 percent). The parliamentary surveys are conducted in ways that make it possible to compare the political views and priorities of politicians with those of voters (the Swedish National Election Studies (SNES) Program). Moreover, the datasets allow for a design that follows developments over time and takes into account a number of factors besides party affiliation and gender. All chapters will include secondary analyses built on data from other parliaments and legislatures. When relevant, worldwide comparisons built on data from the Quality of Government Institute at the Department of Political Science at the University of Gothenburg will be included. The details of the empirical analyses will be presented in the different chapters. Appendix I includes a note on methodology. Moreover, for those with a special interest in Swedish politics, Appendix II includes information on Swedish politics that goes beyond what is needed for the main thread of this book.

The plan for the rest of the book

This book includes empirical research on women, gender, and politics. Equally important, however, is the development of theory; the book will end in a statement of well-founded principles for a gender-sensitive parliament. Chapters 2 and 3 deal with gender-sensitive parties versus gender-sensitive representatives, and lay, together with this introductory chapter, the groundwork for the rest of the book. Chapters 4 to 6 present the bulk of the empirical analyses and focus on the three areas presented previously: internal parliamentary working procedures; room for women's interests and concerns, and the production of gender-sensitive legislation. Chapter 7, the concluding chapter, includes a revised version of the gender-sensitive parliament.

How to take presence theories one step further

Phillips's (1995) book *The Politics of Presence* is a landmark in women and politics research. However, empirical research points out complexities that need to be addressed in new ways. I am primarily thinking of three areas: (i) the role political parties play in mediating legislative behavior and thereby the effects of women's presence in parliaments; (ii) the tension between social background characteristics and intentional group representation; and (iii) the fact that research on outcomes in citizens' everyday lives tends to show that the election of a high number of women has a smaller effect than anticipated in theory.

Chapter 2 focuses on gender-sensitive political parties. Osborn (2012, 6) points out that political parties mediate the effects of women's presence in parliaments in two ways: they organize and present alternatives to address women's interests and concerns, and they create the legislative structure through which these alternatives are considered. More than other scholars in the field, Osborn highlights the fundamental role of political parties in representative democracies. Political parties are, at one and the same time, actors in their own right *and* arenas for conflicting interests. The upshot of this chapter is that parliaments will not change unless major political parties want them to.

Chapter 2 focuses on *parties as collective entities*. I suggest that political parties are different from other organizations in the sense that general elections constitute significant external pressure. Empirical research underpins the notion that processes of self-reflection can start when party competition is high and there is a risk of experiencing noticeable losses (Bækgaard and Jensen 2012). Self-reflection and insight are key factors in self-regulatory processes underpinning the creation of behavioral change. To this chapter I bring those insights into the research on women and politics and suggest that a gender-sensitive political party reflects on gender inequalities and enforces strategies to transform the status of women vis-à-vis men. Through the study of internal party documents I show that, since the 1970s, there has been an ongoing internal debate on gender equality within the major Swedish parties. However, I also suggest that there are differences between parties and time periods. One reason we cannot expect a linear process toward gender equality is that not all actors move at the same speed or in the same direction. Moreover, changes that occur during some periods need to be explained with reference to period-specific events. A case in point is the economic crisis at the beginning of the 1990s, when issues of gender equality were de-prioritized by political actors in Sweden.

In Chapter 3 the focus shifts toward *parties as arenas where conflicting interests encounter each other*. External shocks – exogenous factors – are important for the behavior of parties but so too are endogenous factors – for example, changes that emerge from the gradual replacement of men by women. In this chapter deliberative aspects of representative democracies come to the fore; interests are not set in stone but formed in political debates and negotiations.

Chapter 3 starts with a theoretical definition of the concept of women's interests. The concept is contested, but I believe that self-determination is a useful starting point. To devise more concrete definitions, however, one needs to take context into account. I discuss women's interests in the context of Scandinavian welfare states. This chapter also digs deeper into the role of objective social background characteristics versus the role of intentional group representation. On the theoretical level there seem to be different versions of presence theories – conflicting views are illustrated with reference to studies by Anne Phillips (1995) and Iris Marion Young (2000) – but can we expect this distinction to be of any importance in practice? In sum, Chapter 3 aims to explore what, more exactly, we can expect conflicting interests to be, and who – women or any group-aware representative – we can expect to be a gender-sensitive representative.

Chapter 4 focuses on *internal parliamentary working procedures*. The core question concerns whether women entering the Swedish parliament meet gender-specific obstacles, and if so, how great those obstacles are. In this Chapter I use indicators of formal power positions, such as being a standing committee member or board chair. Patterns of functional divisions between women and men are mapped out and evaluated. I also use indicators of informal power, such as how women and men politicians themselves perceive their ability to make an impact.

Chapter 5 focuses on *the amount of room available for women's interests and concerns*. The first part of the chapter includes an attempt to capture scope and prominence on an institutional, collective level. We shall see, however, that this is easier said than done, and analyses will rely heavily on data generated through questionnaires completed by members of the Swedish parliament. The questionnaire-based data cover information on priorities, attitudes, and policy promotion. The advantage of the questionnaire-based data is that we can conduct rather sophisticated analyses to investigate who is pushing for change that is consistent with women's interests. The data also allow for far-reaching comparisons with priorities and attitudes among citizens. This is important, as responsiveness is a core value in political representation.

The focus in Chapter 6 is on *the production of gender-sensitive legislation*. It was stated previously that this is a matter of measuring "success." This chapter highlights the interplay between parliamentary laws/regulations and actual conditions in citizens' everyday lives. A preliminary way of defining "gender-sensitive legislation" is to say that it covers laws pertaining to women's rights. However, in this chapter I suggest that we need to take two things into account: (i) whether women's situation has to be addressed explicitly for laws/regulations to have a bearing on the status of women vis-à-vis men; and (ii) whether one can expect all types of laws/regulations to be forcefully implemented. At this point I want to stress that this chapter will be a bit more impressionistic than other chapters in the book, as good data on gender-sensitive legislation are scarce. The main objective of Chapter 6 is to analyze transformations in Sweden over time from a comparative perspective. Is it reasonable to believe that the Swedish parliament has played a role in the transformation of Swedish society?

Along with a revised version of the ideas presented so far, the concluding Chapter 7 includes a discussion of how broadly these ideas can be applied: To what extent is it possible to state generally valid principles of a gender-sensitive parliament?

In her book, Anne Phillips (1995) focuses on gender, but she also discusses dimensions of class and ethnicity. However, Phillips is rather vague when it comes to these other categories. For instance, she argues that ethnicity is an even more heterogeneous category than gender, and that the party structure in most liberal democracies is built on class cleavages. The response to this could be that, yes, gender is a special category, but it could also be that the mechanisms at work are quite similar across several different categories. I shall provide some insight into this debate in multiple categories; however, it should be made clear from the start that the focus of the present book is the gender dimension. This choice is primarily based on the desire to do an in-depth study. I shall, in the concluding chapter, discuss whether the framework applied in this book can be used also in the study of other dimensions of representative democracy.

Notes

1 The figure 40 percent came from a review of the membership base within the Liberal Party: 40 percent of the members at that time were women, and so it was reasonable to assume, the argument went, that women should make up 40 percent of members of internal party boards (Wängnerud 2001).
2 The empirical focus in this book is on Sweden, which has a parliamentary system (unicameral). However, the theoretical reasoning should also apply to presidential systems. In the concluding chapter I shall address the question of how broadly these ideas can be applied. So far, I believe that the results are valid for countries that are considered free in terms of established measures of democracy such as those produced by Polity and Freedom House. Throughout the book I shall in most cases refer to "parliaments," the "parliamentary process," and so forth; however, occasionally I refer to "legislatures" or "the legislative process."
3 Statistics Sweden publishes gender-specific data in their report *Women and Men in Sweden: Facts and Figures*, updated regularly. Reports can be found at www.scb.se.
4 These organizations were chosen as they have a good international reputation, and the gender-related indices they produce are frequently referenced. However, all rankings of countries should be interpreted carefully. In Chapter 6 I shall return to a discussion of these indices.
5 This argument is made, for example, by Dahlerup (2006b, 158). See also Wängnerud (2009) for an overview of studies.
6 I build on a tradition established earlier by Sue Thomas (1994), which distinguishes between legislative procedures and legislative products in the study of women in elected office.
7 As of October 1, 2014 (www.ipu.org). The data for Sweden refer to the situation right after the election on September 14, 2014.

Bibliography

Bækgaard, Martin and Carsten Jensen. 2012. "The Dynamics of Competitor Party Behaviour." *Political Studies* 60: 131–146.
Bergqvist, Christina, Anette Borchost, Ann-Dorte Christensen, Viveca Ramstedt-Silén, Nina C. Rauum and Auður Styrkársdóttir. 2000. *Equal Democracies? Gender and Politics in the Nordic Countries*. Oslo: Norwegian University Press.
Bratton, Kathleen A. and Leonard P. Ray. 2002. "Descriptive Representation, Policy Outcomes, and Municipal Day-care Coverage in Norway." *American Journal of Political Science* 46(2): 428–437.

Celis, Karen. 2006. "Substantive Representation of Women: The Representation of Women's Interests and the Impact of Descriptive Representation in the Belgian Parliament (1900–1979)." *Journal of Women, Politics & Policy* 28(2): 85–114.

Celis, Karen and Sarah Childs. 2008. "Introduction: The Descriptive and Substantive Representation of Women: New Directions." *Parliamentary Affairs* 61(3): 419–425.

Dahlerup, Drude. 1988. "From a Small to a Large Minority: Women in Scandinavian Politics." *Scandinavian Political Studies* 11(4): 275–298.

Dahlerup, Drude. 2006a. "The Story of the Theory of Critical Mass." *Politics & Gender* 2(4): 511–522.

Dahlerup, Drude, ed. 2006b. *Women, Quotas and Politics*. London: Routledge.

Dahlerup, Drude and Monique Leyenaar, eds. 2013. *Breaking Male Dominance in Old Democracies*. Oxford: Oxford University Press.

Dodson, Deborah L. 2006. *The Impact of Women in Congress*. Oxford: Oxford University Press.

Freidenvall, Lenita. 2006. *Vägen till Varannan Damernas. Om kvinnorepresentation, kvotering och kandidaturval i svensk politik 1970–2002*. Stockholm: University of Stockholm, Department of Political Science.

Grey, Sandra. 2006. "Numbers and Beyond: The Relevance of Critical Mass in Gender Research." *Politics & Gender* 2(4): 492–502.

Hernes, Helga. 1987. *Welfare State and Woman Power: Essays in State Feminism*. Oslo: Oslo Norwegian Press.

Htun, Mala and Laurel S. Weldon. 2012. "The Civic Origins of Progressive Policy Change: Combating Violence Against Women in Global Perspective, 1975–2005." *American Political Science Review* 106(3): 548–569.

Inglehart, Ronald and Pippa Norris. 2003. *Rising Tide: Gender Equality and Cultural Change Around the World*. Cambridge: Cambridge University Press.

Kittilson, Miki C.. 2006. *Challenging Parties, Changing Parliaments. Women and Elected Office in Contemporary Western Europe*. Columbus: Ohio State University Press.

Krook, Mona Lena and Sarah Childs. 2010. *Women, Gender and Politics: A Reader*. New York: Oxford University Press.

Lovenduski, Joni. 2005. *Feminizing Politics*. Cambridge: Polity Press.

Lovenduski, Joni and Marika Guadagnini. 2010. "Political Representation." In *The Politics of State Feminism: Innovation in Comparative Research*, ed. Dorothy E. McBride and Amy G. Mazur. Philadelphia, PA: Temple University Press, pp. 164–192.

McBride, Dorothy E. and Amy G. Mazur. 2010. *The Politics of State Feminism: Innovation in Comparative Research*. Philadelphia, PA: Temple University Press.

Norris, Pippa. 2005. *Radical Right: Voters and Parties on the Electoral Market*. Cambridge: Cambridge University Press.

Osborn, Tracy L. 2012. *How Women Represent Women: Political Parties, Gender, and Representation in the State Legislatures*. New York: Oxford University Press.

Phillips, Anne. 1991. *Engendering Democracy*. University Park: Pennsylvania University Press.

Phillips, Anne. 1995. *The Politics of Presence*. Oxford: Oxford University Press.

Phillips, Anne. 2007. *Multiculturalism Without Culture*. Princeton, NJ: Princeton University Press.

Pitkin, Hanna F. 1967. *The Concept of Representation*. Berkeley: University of California Press.

Saward, Michael. 2010. *The Representative Claim*. Oxford: Oxford University Press.

Schwindt-Bayer, Leslie A. and William Mishler. 2005. "An Integrated Model of Women's Representation." *Journal of Politics* 67(2): 407–428.
Skjeie, Hege. 1992. *Den politiske betydningen av kjønn. En studie av norsk topp-politikk.* Oslo: Institutt for Samfunnsforskning, rapport 92.11.
Thomas, Susan. 1994. *How Women Legislate.* Oxford: Oxford University Press.
Wängnerud, Lena. 2000. "Testing the Politics of Presence: Women's Representation in the Swedish Riksdag." *Scandinavian Political Studies* 23(1): 67–91.
Wängnerud, Lena. 2001. "Kvinnors röst: En kamp mellan partier." In *Rösträtten 80 år. Forskarantologi*, ed. Christer Jönsson. Stockholm: Justitiedepartementet.
Wängnerud, Lena. 2009. "Women in Parliaments: Descriptive and Substantive Representation." *Annual Review of Political Science* 12: 51–69.
Wängnerud, Lena and Anders Sundell. 2012. "Do Politics Matter? Women in Swedish Local Elected Assemblies 1970–2010 and Gender Equality in Outcomes." *European Political Science Review* 4(01): 97–120.
Yoo, Eunhye. 2012. "The Impact of Domestic and Transnational Conditions." *Politics & Gender* 8: 304–340.
Young, Iris M. 2000. *Inclusion and Democracy.* Oxford: Oxford University Press.

2 Gender-sensitive political parties

In representative democracies political parties are the main actors. They not only control the recruitment process – who gets elected – but also internal parliamentary processes. Tracy Osborn (2012, 6) has pointed out that political parties mediate the effects of women's presence in parliaments in two ways: they organize and present alternatives to address women's issues and concerns, and they create the legislative structure through which these alternatives are considered.

To understand fully how political parties mediate the effect of women's presence in parliaments, we need to study their commitment to gender equality. Dahlerup and Leyenaar (2013, 232) state that, in comparison to a number of other "old" democracies, Sweden is the country that comes closest to a model of gender parity. They underpin their conclusion with the facts that women usually constitute half of the ministers in Sweden; that there have been several female speakers in the Riksdag; and that women are almost 50 percent in the Riksdag and, on average, more than 40 percent in local councils. Moreover, they note that all but a few political parties have inscribed not just gender equality but even feminism in their party programs (ibid.).

Dahlerup and Leyenaar (2013, 233) remind us that parity in numbers does not remove all barriers for women politicians. Still, analyses relying on official documents and statistics tend to produce a rather rosy picture of the Swedish case. Most important is that official documents and statistics are insufficient if we want to capture commitments to gender equality in the everyday lives of political parties. The point of departure for this chapter is that party ideologies change over time and that these changes have a bearing on processes related to gender equality. To study ideological shifts I shall rely on the Swedish Parliamentary Surveys, presented in Chapter 1. These surveys include not only questions on ideological position but also questions on attitudes toward gender equality – why there should be an equal distribution of women and men in parliament. Thus, we are able to move beyond more conventional studies of official documents and display gender-related norms through the minds of elected representatives.

The focus of the following analyses is not on commitments or norms in their own right. The upshot of this chapter is that parliaments will not change unless major political parties want them to. Thus, the critical question is, *Do political parties want parliaments to change?* The phenomenon in focus is understandings of gender equality that may have an effect on outcomes (Hawkesworth 2005). We know that parliamentary processes can never be planned entirely in advance. This means that elected representatives have room to maneuver, and party programs should not be seen as detailed descriptions on how to behave. In this chapter we shall get a sense of how pervasive publicly stated commitments to gender equality are.

The first step of this chapter is to present a bird's-eye view of women's descriptive representation in Sweden. Thereafter, we shall move on to an analysis of the political parties' commitment to gender equality and a more thorough discussion of the meaning of a gender-sensitive political party.

A bird's-eye view of women's descriptive representation in Sweden

This book started with a citation from Gunnar Helén, the former leader of the Liberal Party in Sweden. Helén criticized Olof Palme, the former leader of the Social Democratic Party, for his lack of concrete proposals concerning gender equality. The more common way to start an exposé of Swedish politics from a gender perspective is to start from the other end, with the groundbreaking speech by Palme. In 1972 Palme was not only the leader of the Social Democratic Party but also the prime minister of Sweden. The speech had, without doubt, a strong signal effect – gender equality was no longer to be seen as a concern for women only or for the women's branch of the Social Democratic Party, but for society as a whole (Karlsson 1996; Sainsbury 1993, 281).

The reason to start with Helén's reaction to Palme's speech is, however, to highlight the competition that started between two major political players at that time. The events of 1972 – Helén and Palme's confrontation – had a prelude. In Sweden, women gained universal suffrage through constitutional reform in 1919–21. The road that led to franchise was paved not only with protests and campaigns targeting decision makers but also with mobilization efforts targeting women (Rönnbäck 2004). However, in the first national election in which women could participate on equal terms with men, there was a rather big gender gap in turnout: 62 percent of men but only 47 percent of women used their right to vote, which corresponds to a gap of 15 percentage points. In the 1940s the gap had diminished to below 10 percentage points, but at the end of the 1960s the gap had still not closed (Oskarson and Wängnerud 2013, 69).[1] Moreover, during the 1960s more women than men voted for the Conservative Party (Oscarsson and Holmberg 2008, 332). This formed the breeding ground for strategic considerations within the Liberal Party and the Social Democratic Party. In short, if they could mobilize more women to vote and also win over women from the

Conservative Party, this would make them into bigger, even more powerful parties.[2]

Proof of strategic reasoning in party documents

Richard Matland and Donley Studlar (1996) have suggested a theory of "contagion effects," which means that once a party in a given system starts to politicize issues of women's representation, other political parties within that system will follow suit. One needs to consider the question of *why* other political parties will follow suit. The obvious answer is that the *raison d'être* for political parties is to gain power, and gender equality can be one weapon, among others, to reach that goal.

I have collected internal party documents for the major political parties in Sweden for the period 1970–98.[3] These documents are comparatively rich in references to "gender equality," "women's representation," "the women's issues," and similar concepts, but these matters are most often discussed in ideological language. On some occasions, however, it is possible to find proof of strategic reasoning among key actors. One especially convincing example of strategic reasoning, emphasizing the need to become a bigger party, is to be found in a report to the Liberal Party Congress in 1971. In the report, *Justice for Women*, it is stated:

> Only 11–12% of Liberal Party voters are affiliated to the party. Despite recruitment, membership has declined because of high attrition. It relies on those of high average age. The party needs especially younger and more female members.

This is the background for the attack by Helén on Palme previously described. Both parties could not, at least not with the same success, win the female vote. Documents from the Social Democratic Party Congress 1972 show that the party leadership was concerned; they asked party members to support a "systematic inventory to increase the number of politically active women."

The analysis of internal party documents shows that the most explicit examples of strategic reasoning are found in documents from the beginning of the 1970s and also from the period around the end of the 1980s/beginning of the 1990s. For example, in 1990 the national board of the Conservative Party stated, "It is important that the relationship 'significantly fewer women than men vote for the Conservative Party' is smoothed." The board refers to results from studies on gender gaps in party choice in Sweden. In the 1990s more men than women voted for the Conservative Party. A motion to the Social Democratic Party Congress in 1993 stated, "Our party cannot do without women's continued voter support. We should not risk them [women] leaving us and being attracted by pure women's parties." In that same year, the board of the Left Party stated in a document to the Left

Party Congress that, "The political parties currently have a choice. To pull themselves together or let a women's party grow. Our party has hardly anything to gain from the latter." As early as 1988 the Green Party had anticipated a threat from a women's party. In a motion to the Green Party Congress a member suggested a separate women's list for the upcoming election:

> I am convinced that we can get votes on a women's parliamentary list that we would not otherwise get. So, I think we would, in total, get more votes to parliament when we have both versions [of the list] side by side. If we get a women's party standing for parliament the women's list becomes even more important.

I believe that these proofs of strategic reasoning are important. They show that the topic of gender equality is tied to core interests – the striving for power – of political parties. In terms of concrete strategies, the 1970s was an era of "soft quotas" in Sweden; all major political parties adopted recommendations and goal formulations to speed up the processes. In 1987 the Social Democratic Party decided that there should be "a minimum of 40 percent of each sex on party lists." In the same year, the Left Party decided that there should be "as many women on party lists as female party members," and the Green Party, also in 1987, had made a decision that "the party lists are to be gender balanced" (Freidenvall 2013, 109). In the late 1980s an era began in which three parties were moving toward a strict gender quota.

The number of women elected

In 1970 the upper chamber was abolished in Sweden. The introduction of a one-chamber system was accompanied by the introduction of a 4 percent electoral threshold. Thus, the rules of the game were changed, and instead of providing 151 members to the upper chamber and 233 members to the lower chamber, the political parties were asked to provide 350 members to one chamber (later changed to 349 members). Taken together, these changes constituted a new, more uncertain situation for the political parties.

Empirical research shows that processes of self-reflection leading to behavioral change can start when party competition is high and there is a risk of experiencing losses (Bækgaard and Jensen 2012). The early 1970s were indeed competitive. In addition to the indicators already discussed, it should be noted that the Social Democratic Party had experienced noticeable losses in the 1970 election (from 50 to 45 percent of the vote). The Liberal Party gained some votes in the same election (from 14 to 16 percent), but compared to its heyday in the 1950s, when the Liberal Party was supported by almost 25 percent of the Swedish electorate, the 1970 election was a disappointment.

Figure 2.1 shows the number of women in the Swedish parliament from 1971–2014. The results show that the 1973 election resulted in a significantly higher proportion of women: the number went up from 14 to 21 percent. Moreover, the results in Figure 2.1 show that a corresponding increase has only occurred on one other occasion, and that was in the 1994 election, when the proportion of women went up from 34 to 41 percent.

The most striking result in Figure 2.1 is perhaps the *decrease*, from 38 to 34 percent, that occurred in the election of 1991. This decrease coincided with a shift in government, from a Social Democratic government to a coalition formed by center-right parties. For the first time in modern Swedish history a right-wing populist party, New Democracy, gained seats in the Riksdag in that election. Soon after the election some influential journalists and academics came forward as leaders for a loosely formed feminist network called the Support Stockings. The network brought forward the demand of "half the power, all the salary," focusing on wage discrimination and the scarcity of women in elite positions in society (Eduards 2002, 67–73; Freidenvall 2006, 130).

The activities of the feminist network should be seen against the backdrop of the economic recession in the early 1990s. Reports were published in Sweden demonstrating that single mothers were one of the groups hardest hit by cutbacks and rearrangements of the welfare state (Palme et al. 2001 provide an overview). Moreover, in 1990 the much-noticed *Swedish Power Investigation* was published. In this government report the historian Yvonne Hirdman (1990) argued that Sweden was characterized by a gender system in

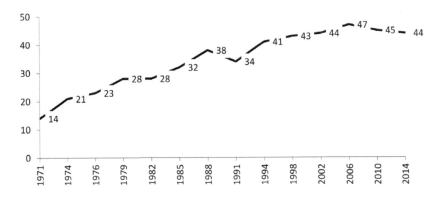

Figure 2.1 Number of women in the Swedish parliament, 1971–2014 (%)
The number of members of parliament (MPs) was 350 in 1971 and 1974, and 349 thereafter. Until 1994 the term was three years, and thereafter four years. Elections were held in 1970 and 1973; however, the newly elected Riksdag assembled in January of the following year. In 1976 this was changed, and the newly elected Riksdag has, since then, assembled in close connection to the elections. The figure reports percentages right after the election.
(Statistics Sweden)

which women, in spite of formal rights, were subordinated to men. Hirdman's analysis provoked intense public debate, as it collided with the prevailing picture, at that time, of Sweden as the international forerunner in the field of gender equality and the idea of gender equality as a linear process.

All told, the elements of recession, the decrease in the proportion of women in parliament, and a changing public discourse on gender equality constituted what could be called a "window of opportunity" for radical feminism in Sweden (Teigen and Wängnerud 2009). In January 1994, about six months before election day, opinion polls showed that 23 percent of Swedish voters were prepared to vote for a women's party, and 15 percent would like to see Maria-Pia Boëthius – one of the spokeswomen for the Support Stockings – as Sweden's prime minister (Ulmanen 1998, 51). The Support Stockings threatened to form a feminist party, but in the end this threat was not carried out. However, all major political parties in Sweden made adaptations to the network's demand of "half the power," and in the 1994 election the proportion of women in the Riksdag increased to 41 percent (Figure 2.1). The Support Stockings was disbanded shortly after the election.

The effect of exogenous factors

The story told above is one in which party competition and exogenous factors such as constitutional changes and the formation of a feminist network affected political parties' willingness to put women forward. In the late 1980s party competition in Sweden was heightened by the entrance of new parties: the Green Party entered the parliament for the first time in the 1988 election, and the Christian Democratic Party and New Democracy in 1991. In less than a decade the once-stable five-party system in Sweden had changed to an eight-party system (Demker and Svåsand 2005).

It is reasonable to assign weight to factors exogenous to political parties. We have seen that three parties – the Social Democratic Party, the Left Party, and the Green Party – adopted comparatively strict rules for the gender composition of party lists even in 1987. It was, however, not until the 1994 election that these parties reached a balance of women and men in their respective party groups. Table 2.1 shows the number of women in parliamentary party groups in Sweden in 1985–2014. In the election of 2010 a new right-wing populist party, the Sweden Democrats, entered the Riksdag.[4]

Taking a bird's-eye view of developments in Sweden, the theory of contagion effects (Matland and Studlar 1996) is suitable for the Swedish case until the 1990s. In the early 1970s two of the major political players in Sweden were, as already discussed, the Social Democratic Party and the Liberal Party, and they took the lead, introducing strategies that accelerated the descriptive representation of women. Soon, other parties followed suit and adopted recommendations and goal formulations to increase the number of women elected (Freidenvall 2006). However, in the 1990s a new situation emerged. Left-green parties had moved toward a stricter quota

Table 2.1 The number of women in parliamentary party groups in Sweden, 1985–2014 (%)

Year	Left-green parties				Center-right parties				Right populist parties	
	Lft	SocDem	Grn	Cen	Lib	ChrDem	Con	NewDem	SweDem
1985	16	35	–	32	39	–	22	–	–
1988	38	41	45	38	43	–	27	–	–
1991	31	41	–	39	33	31	26	12	–
1994	46	48	56	37	35	33	28	–	–
1998	42	50	50	56	35	41	30	–	–
2002	47	48	59	50	48	30	40	–	–
2006	64	50	53	38	50	46	43	–	–
2010	58	48	56	39	38	42	48	–	15
2014	57	46	48	41	26	38	52	–	22

(Parliamentary membership rolls)

The table reports percentages after the appointment of parliamentary speaker and cabinet ministers. A list of the abbreviations used for the parties can be found on p. ix.

system, and the gray shading in Table 2.1 shows that since the 1994 election all of these parties have had more than 40 percent women in their parliamentary party groups (this is not the case in center-right parties). In the 1990s the political landscape had shifted in Sweden, and now the two major players were the Social Democratic Party and the Conservative Party. In the next section we shall see how pervasive this shift was.

Tracing ideological changes

Why party ideology changes is a research field in itself. I shall restrict myself to describing changes in the past three decades and linking them to processes related to gender equality. The Swedish Parliamentary Surveys include a question on subjective left–right ideology. MPs are asked to place themselves on a scale from 0 (far left) to 10 (far right). Figure 2.2 shows mean values within parties from 1985 to 2010. Through this lens we can trace ideological shifts in the Swedish party system.

The results in Figure 2.2 show several important things: First, if we look at the results for 1985 we see a five-party system with three distinct blocs: *the left*, consisting of the Left Party and the Social Democratic Party; *the middle*, consisting of the Center Party and the Liberal Party; and *the right*, consisting of the Conservative Party. This result symbolizes the five-party system that dominated the political scene in Sweden for more than 50 years.

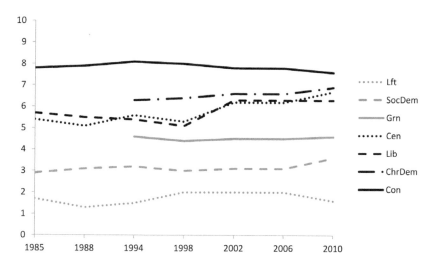

Figure 2.2 Subjective left–right self-placement by Swedish MPs, 1985–2010
The figure shows mean values within parties on an 11-point scale from 0 (far left) to 10 (far right). In 2010 Sweden Democrats are found at 6.0 (not shown). Note that there was no survey following the 1991 election.
(Swedish Parliamentary Surveys, Department of Political Science, University of Gothenburg)

Over time more parties have entered the scene, but most important to note in Figure 2.2 is how the middle parties – the Center Party and the Liberal Party – have moved toward the right in their ideological positioning. After the 2002 election it is reasonable to talk about two distinct blocs in Sweden,[5] with on the one hand *the left-green* bloc consisting of the Left Party, the Social Democratic Party, and the Green Party, and on the other hand, *the center-right* bloc consisting of the Conservative Party, the Christian Democratic Party, the Center Party, and the Liberal Party. The right-wing populist parties in Sweden, New Democracy in 1991, and the Sweden Democrats in 2010 and 2014, have never been part of any serious collaborations, and therefore cannot be said to belong to any bloc in the Riksdag.

Ideological shifts and commitments to gender equality

How to capture political parties' commitment to gender equality is a tricky question. The reason for trying, however, is the important role that political parties play in the effect of women's presence in parliament. Scholarship on feminist institutionalism argues that institutions are gendered – that is, they produce rules about gender and shape the behavior of individual women and men (Chappell and Waylen 2013; Hawkesworth 2005; Krook and Mackay 2010). For MPs, the most important institution is their own party group. Formal rules for elected representatives are set by constitutions, electoral laws, and parliamentary regulations, but institutions are also seen as imposing *informal* rules affecting actors' behavior by influencing the norms and understandings taken for granted (March and Olsen 1989). Following this line of reasoning, the notion of political parties as arenas for gender-related production of norms needs to be scrutinized.

Previous scholarship on gender norms has focused to a large extent on national characteristics. In cross-country comparative research Sweden and the other Nordic countries are regularly singled out as highly gender-egalitarian societies (Graubard 1986; Inglehart and Norris 2003). Nordic scholars have differentiated between different "frames" or "discourses" within this egalitarian context. One example is a study by Anette Borchorst, Ann-Dorthe Christensen, and Birte Siim (2002), which focuses on the academic discourses on gender, politics, and power in Denmark, Norway, and Sweden. Based on their results, they differentiate between a discourse on gender differences (Norway), a discourse on women's subordination (Sweden), and a discourse on empowerment in which women are seen as gaining ground vis-à-vis men (Denmark). In a similar vein, Dahlerup (2002) analyzes discourses in political party programs in Sweden and Denmark, and concludes that gender equality is more highly politicized in Swedish, compared with Danish, political life. Dahlerup states that there seems to be a competition among Swedish parties, not only regarding the number of women elected, but also regarding who is most "feminist."

Analyses like the ones presented above have led scholars to suggest that gender equality is an institutionalized norm in Swedish politics (cf. Dahlerup and Leyenaar 2013, 233), but there are good reasons to try to capture understandings of gender equality through other, less official sources than party programs. Key here is whether one believes that there are certain underlying norms that may affect the behavior of individuals, in this case male and female elected representatives. It is quite evident that Swedish political parties are, in their rhetoric, committed to gender equality, but informal norms can sometimes contradict official statements.

Tracing norms of gender equality through the minds of elected representatives

Swedish MPs have been asked to evaluate a number of future societies such as an environmentally oriented society, a society in which Christian values play a more important role, a socialist society, and so forth. In 1994 the list of future societies contained a question on MPs' attitudes toward the suggestion "to work toward a society with more equality between women and men." MPs were asked to place themselves on a scale from 0 (very bad proposal) to 10 (very good proposal). The results show little variation between groups of MPs and, in comparison with other future societies, strikingly positive attitudes: The average mean among women MPs was 9.6 and among men MPs 8.2 (Oskarson and Wängnerud 1996). These results strengthen the idea of institutionalized gender equality in Swedish politics.

Judith Squires (1999) has suggested that it is possible to distinguish between ideas and strategies of *inclusion* versus ideas and strategies of *reversal* in processes related to gender equality. Strategies of inclusion are often defended by liberal feminists and aim at the inclusion of women in the world "as it is." It is the exclusion of women that is problematized. Strategies of reversal are more often defended by radical feminists and aim at transformations of current politics, so that it becomes more open to gendered specifications (see also Verloo 2005, 346).[6]

The following analysis of political parties' commitments to gender equality is based on this distinction between inclusive and transformative elements. If one is looking for commitments that may matter for behavior, it should be meaningful to try to capture the extent to which political parties embrace inclusive and/or transformative ways of thinking. Since 1994 the Swedish Parliamentary Surveys have included a question on different arguments for an equal distribution of women and men in the parliament. The argument that "the composition of parliament should reflect the most important groups in society" is used to measure a norm of inclusion, whereas the argument that "there will be consequences for policies" is used to measure a norm of reversal. For each argument, respondents have been asked to assess whether they perceive the argument to be "very important," "fairly important," "not very important," or "not at all important." Figure 2.3 reports the number answering "very important" as an argument in the Riksdag as a whole.

The first thing to notice in Figure 2.3 is that the support for both arguments is high. In fact, if one takes into account respondents answering "fairly important," the first argument is supported by almost 90 percent of Swedish MPs. The proportions answering "very important" are, for the first argument, 54 percent in 1994 and 48 percent in 2010. For the second argument the proportions answering "very important" are 26 percent in 1994 and 26 percent in 2010.

The second thing to notice in Figure 2.3 is that there seems to be little fluctuation over time. The only noticeable trend in Figure 2.3 is that support for the first argument decreased slightly between 1994 and 2010. Using regression analysis, we shall, however, see variation across time and across political parties. Behind the seemingly stable situation displayed in Figure 2.3 dramatic changes are taking place.

Table 2.2 includes results from a multivariate regression which, besides party affiliation, includes MPs' gender, and also the variables of age, parliamentary experience, education, and whether the MPs hold a distinguished power position such as being a chair of a standing committee, a member of the party board, or similar. (These control variables will be used throughout

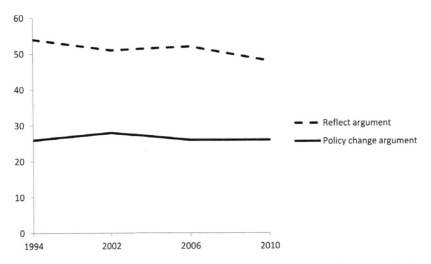

Figure 2.3 Attitudes among Swedish MPs toward two arguments for an equal distribution of women and men in the parliament, 1994–2010 (% "very important")

The question reads, "There are various ways to argue for an equal distribution of women and men in the Riksdag. How important do you consider the following argument to be? (1) The composition of parliament should reflect the most important groups in society. (2) There will be consequences for policies." The following response alternatives were offered: "very important," "fairly important," "not very important," "not at all important."

(Swedish Parliamentary Surveys, Department of Political Science, University of Gothenburg)

Gender-sensitive political parties 29

the book, and they are explained in Appendix I.) In the multivariate regression the Conservative Party is used as a reference category. This is because previous studies have shown that the Conservative Party used to be less enthusiastic about gender equality than other political parties in Sweden (Wängnerud 2000a). The dependent variable is a dichotomy that distinguishes between respondents answering "very important" and the rest, meaning that the categories "fairly important," "not very important," and "not at all important" have been merged.[7]

Table 2.2 includes results for 1994 and 2010, and through the comparison of these two points we are able to see developments. Gender is significant on both survey occasions and for the analysis of both arguments, which means that more women than men answer that it is a "very important" argument that the composition of parliament should reflect the most important groups in society, and a "very important" argument that there will be consequences for policies. The most noticeable changes take place among center-right parties. In 1994 all other parties in the Riksdag are significantly different from the Conservative Party, and this result is valid for both arguments (meaning that MPs within the Conservative Party are less supportive of each argument than MPs in other parties). In 2010 it is only the left-green parties that are significantly different from the Conservative Party in the analyses of both arguments. This means that the center-right parties, over time, are becoming more alike, which could be expected if one considers the changes on the subjective left–right dimension previously displayed in Figure 2.3.[8]

Figure 2.4 includes the proportion answering "very important" to the argument in the four center-right parties 1994–2010. This figure is a visualization of the main results in the multivariate regression.

If we consider previous descriptions, in which the Liberal Party in Sweden has been ascribed a leading role in processes related to gender equality, the trend for this party becomes the most surprising result in Figure 2.4. For both arguments there is a clear downward trend between 1994 and 2010. This result should be contrasted with the upward trend within the Conservative Party, found in the analyses of both arguments. For the Center Party, support for the first (reflect) argument remains high over time, whereas support for the second (policy change) argument loses support. For the Christian Democratic Party the most noticeable result is that the second argument gains support over time. All in all, the major finding is that the center-right parties are becoming more alike and that the left-green parties, with minor exceptions, display higher levels of support for both arguments on all survey occasions (results for the left-green parties are not reported in a figure).

Comparing Swedish and Danish MPs

Before I wrap up the results and provide a more thorough discussion of the meaning of a gender-sensitive party, let us compare Swedish and Danish MPs. The question about different arguments for an equal distribution of women and

Table 2.2 Determinants of attitudes among Swedish MPs toward two arguments for an equal distribution of women and men in parliament, 1994 and 2010 (logistic regression)

	First argument			Second argument		
	B	SE	Sig.	B	SE	Sig.
1994						
Gender	1.42	0.29	0.00	2.43	0.35	0.00
Lft	2.04	0.61	0.00	2.38	0.78	0.00
SocDem	2.29	0.41	0.00	1.85	0.60	0.00
Grn	1.96	0.69	0.00	3.37	0.88	0.00
Cen	2.31	0.55	0.00	1.91	0.75	0.01
Lib	1.81	0.55	0.00	2.53	0.74	0.00
ChrDem	1.94	0.70	0.00	–	–	–
Con (reference)						
Age	0.00	0.01	0.74	0.01	0.02	0.52
Experience	0.00	0.02	0.84	-0.26	0.03	0.43
Education	-0.38	0.29	0.18	0.00	0.33	0.99
Power position	-0.20	0.32	0.52	-0.68	0.39	0.08
Constant	-1.64	0.99	0.09	-4.37	1.25	0.00
Nagelkerke	0.32			0.42		
2010						
Gender	0.44	0.27	0.10	1.28	0.31	0.00
Lft	1.73	0.60	0.00	1.53	0.63	0.01
SocDem	1.12	0.36	0.00	1.84	0.44	0.00
Grn	1.69	0.54	0.00	1.24	0.60	0.04
Cen	1.69	0.59	0.00	0.25	0.85	0.76
Lib	0.08	0.57	0.88	1.08	0.66	0.10
ChrDem	0.56	0.57	0.32	1.2	0.66	0.07
SweDem	-1.26	1.11	0.25	–	–	–
Con (reference)						
Age	0.02	0.01	0.12	0.03	0.01	0.05
Experience	0.00	0.02	0.99	-0.05	0.03	0.10
Education	-0.34	0.33	0.29	0.25	0.36	0.49
Power position	-0.65	0.31	0.03	-0.51	0.36	0.15
Constant	-1.51	0.77	0.05	-3.96	0.94	0.00
Nagelkerke	0.19			0.25		

(Swedish Parliamentary Surveys, Department of Political Science, University of Gothenburg)

See Figure 2.3 for the question asked and the two arguments. The dependent variable is a dichotomy between respondents answering "very important" and the other categories combined ("fairly important," "not very important," and "not at all important"). See the Appendices for information on the different control variables.

Gender-sensitive political parties 31

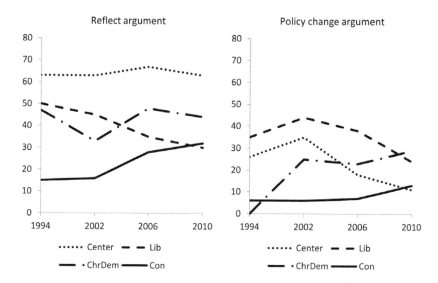

Figure 2.4 Attitudes toward two arguments for an equal distribution of women and men in parliament among MPs in center-right political parties, 1994–2010 (% "very important")
See Figure 2.3 for the question asked and the two arguments.
(Swedish Parliamentary Surveys, Department of Political Science, University of Gothenburg)

men in the parliament was asked in parliamentary surveys in both countries in 1994 (Sweden and Denmark), and in 2008 (Denmark) and 2010 (Sweden). Figure 2.5 shows the number answering "very important," divided according to women and men MPs in each country.

What stands out as a striking result in Figure 2.5 is that the second (policy change) argument receives much stronger support among women MPs in Sweden than in any other group in 1994 as well as in 2010. Squires (1999) suggests that a strategy of reversal is more often defended by radical feminists and aims at transformations of current politics. If we accept that the second argument is a valid measure of norms of reversal, the results in Figure 2.5 indicate that female politicians in Sweden are particularly imbued with radical feminist ideas.

Several results in Figure 2.5 are worthy of attention. For example, women MPs in both countries are more supportive of both arguments than are their male colleagues. Moreover, the slight decrease in Sweden for the first (reflect) argument, previously discussed in connection with Figure 2.4, is not visible in the Danish case. In 2010 this argument attracts higher support among Danish than Swedish MPs; however, this is not true for the second argument.

Squires (1999) contends that the two approaches to gender equality discussed here are not mutually exclusive, but can be (and are) combined in practice. Additional analyses of the questionnaire-based data confirm that

32 Gender-sensitive political parties

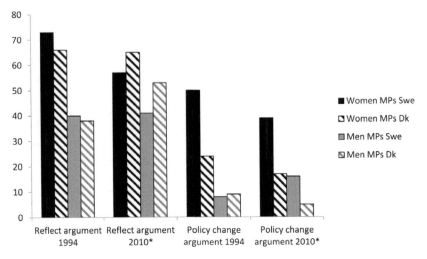

Figure 2.5 Comparing Swedish and Danish MPs: attitudes toward two different arguments for an equal distribution of women and men, 1994 and 2010 (% "very important")
*Data for Denmark from 2008. See Figure 2.3 for the question asked and the two arguments.
(For data on 1994, see Wängnerud 2000b; otherwise, Swedish Parliamentary Survey 2010, and Danish Parliamentary Survey 2008, Department of Political Science, University of Gothenburg)

this is also the case among Swedish and Danish MPs; respondents who score highly on one argument tend also to score highly on the other.

Gender equality in the everyday lives of political parties

Swedish political parties are committed to gender equality. All indicators show that the major parties want the Riksdag to change: they have adopted strategies to increase the number of women elected, and survey-based data show support for the suggestion "to work toward a society with more equality between women and men" as well as for various arguments for an equal distribution of women and men in parliament. Nevertheless, assuming that there is a common "gender-equality standard" that permeates everyday life in the Riksdag leads to erroneous conclusions.

The core survey question used in this chapter measures attitudes toward various arguments for an equal distribution of women and men in parliament. I want to stress that the question is general; it does not concern any concrete policy, and thus it can be assumed to capture underlying norms. There are, however, always trade-offs in research, and the question used does not capture all possible understandings of gender equality. The analyses in this chapter have revealed *dominant* norms in the Riksdag, and how they change over time.

I shall not, at this early stage, stretch the conclusions too far, but we have seen that while the center-right parties have converged on the left–right dimension, they have also become more alike in their approach to gender equality. The dominant norm in center-right parties is that gender equality has to do with inclusion. Inclusion is also the dominant norm in left-green parties, but here there is a stronger element of transformative ideas. Summing up, all major political parties in Sweden can, so far, be classified as gender sensitive, but in slightly different ways.[9]

An objection to the analyses in this chapter could be that the measurements focus on descriptive representation of women and not on gender equality in a broad sense. This is true, and in the concluding chapter we shall get back to a discussion on whether the concepts and indicators used need to be refined in significant ways. Forthcoming analyses will show whether the variation found in this chapter has any bearing on the dimensions of a gender-sensitive parliament outlined in Chapter 1. One preliminary hypothesis could be that forthcoming analyses will find small effects of party affiliation in analyses of internal parliamentary working procedures, since inclusion is a strong commitment among all the major political parties in Sweden. Another preliminary hypothesis could be that effects of party affiliation will be found in the analyses of room for women's interests and concerns, since this dimension builds on the idea brought forward by Phillips (1995), that gender equality among those elected to office is desirable because of the changes it can bring about. For the third dimension of a gender-sensitive parliament, the production of gender-sensitive legislation, it is more difficult to predict an outcome based on the results in this chapter.

Notes

1 The gender gap in voting closed in the 1970s. Since the election of 1985 it has been a slightly higher proportion of women than men who vote in Sweden. In the 2010 election 85 percent of women and 84 percent of men voted (Oskarson and Wängnerud 2013, 65).
2 See Appendix II for information on gender gaps in party choice in Sweden 1956–2010. Also the Liberal Party had more women than men voters in the 1960s.
3 This section builds on Wängnerud (2001, 132–33).
4 The label "right-wing populist" for these two parties can certainly be discussed: their roots are different, but what unites them is, for example, criticism of immigration and anti-establishment rhetoric.
5 Following the 2002 election, the four center-right parties – the Center Party, the Liberal Party, the Christian Democratic Party, and the Conservative Party – formed the Alliance. During the 2006–10 and 2010–14 parliamentary terms Sweden was governed by the Alliance coalition, with the leader of the Conservative Party, Fredrik Reinfeldt, as prime minister. After the election on September 14, 2014, the Social Democratic Party and the Green Party formed a minority government. The Conservative Party made big losses in the 2014 election and Fredrik Reinfeldt resigned. In January 2015 Anna Kinberg Batra was elected as party leader for the Conservative Party. The future of the Alliance coalition was, after the 2014 election, uncertain.

6 Squires (1999) suggests a third strategy, namely, the strategy of displacement, which aspires to move beyond gender and espouse a diversity politics. This strategy is rooted in postmodern or poststructuralist feminism.
7 The reason for merging these categories is that very few respondents use the response alternatives "not very important" or "not at all important."
8 None of the other control variables included in the multivariate regression produces any clear and easily interpretable result, and therefore they are not discussed in this chapter.
9 The populist-right parties, New Democracy and the Sweden Democrats, have only been represented in the Riksdag for short periods. Therefore, it is hard to say much about their understanding of gender equality. However, it is evident that they have very few women in leading positions (see Table 2.1).

Bibliography

Bækgaard, Martin and Carsten Jensen. 2012. "The Dynamics of Competitor Party Behaviour." *Political Studies* 60: 131–146.
Borchorst, Anette, Ann-Dorthe Christensen and Birte Siim. 2002. "Diskurser om køn, magt og politik i Skandinavien." In *Kønsmagt under forandring*, ed. Anette Borchorst. Copenhagen: Hans Reizels Forlag.
Chappell, Louise and Georgina Waylen. 2013. "Gender and the Hidden Life of Institutions." *Public Administration* 91(3): 599–615.
Dahlerup, Drude. 2002. "Er ligestillingen opnået? Ligestillingsdebattens forskjellighed i Danmark og Sverige." In *Kønsmagt under forandring*, ed. Anette Borchorst. Copenhagen: Hans Reitzels Forlag.
Dahlerup, Drude and Monique Leyenaar, eds. 2013. *Breaking Male Dominance in Old Democracies*. Oxford: Oxford University Press.
Demker, Marie and Lars Svåsand, eds. 2005. *Partiernas århundrade. Fempartimodellens uppgång och fall i Norge och Sverige*. Stockholm: Santérus Förlag.
Eduards, Maud. 2002. *Förbjuden handling*. Stockholm: Liber.
Freidenvall, Lenita. 2006. *Vägen till Varannan damernas*. Stockholm: Stockholm University.
Freidenvall, Lenita. 2013. "Sweden: Step by Step – Women's Inroads into Parliamentary Politics." In *Breaking Male Dominance in Old Democracies*, ed. Drude Dahlerup and Monique Leyenaar. Oxford: Oxford University Press.
Graubard, Stephen R., ed. 1986. *Norden – The Passion for Equality*. Oslo: Norwegian University Press.
Hawkesworth, Mary. 2005. "Engendering Political Science: An Immodest Proposal." *Politics & Gender* 1: 141–156.
Hirdman, Yvonne. 1990. "Genussystemet." In *Demokrati och makt i Sverige. Maktutredningens huvudrapport*. SOU 1990:44. Stockholm: Allmänna Förlaget.
Inglehart, Ronald and Pippa Norris. 2003. *Rising Tide: Gender Equality and Cultural Change Around the World*. Cambridge: Cambridge University Press.
Karlsson, Gunnel. 1996. *Från broderskap till systerskap. Det socialdemokratiska kvinnoförbundets kamp för inflytande och makt i SAP*. Lund: Arkiv Förlag.
Krook, Mona Lena and Fiona Mackay, eds. 2010. *Gender, Politics and Institutions: Towards a Feminist Intuitionalism*. Basingstoke and New York: Palgrave Macmillan.
March, James and Johan P. Olsen. 1989. *Rediscovering Institutions. The Organizational Basis of Politics*. New York: Free Press.

Matland, Richard E. and Donley T. Studlar. 1996. "The Contagion of Women Candidates in Single-Member District and Proportional Representation Electoral Systems: Canada and Norway." *Journal of Politics* 3: 707–733.
Osborn, Tracy L. 2012. *How Women Represent Women: Political Parties, Gender, and Representation in State Legislatures*. Oxford: Oxford University Press.
Oscarsson, Henrik and Sören Holmberg. 2008. *Regeringsskifte. Väljarna och valet 2006*. Stockholm: Norstedts Juridik.
Oskarson, Maria and Lena Wängnerud. 1996. "Vem representerar kvinnorna?" In *Vetenskapen om politik. Festskrift till professor emeritus Jörgen Westerståhl*, ed. Bo Rothstein and Bo Särlvik. Gothenburg: University of Gothenburg.
Oskarson, Maria and Lena Wängnerud. 2013. "The Story of the Gender Gap in Swedish Politics: Only Partially Diminishing Differences." In *Stepping Stones: Research on Political Representation, Voting Behavior, and Quality of Government*, ed. Stefan Dahlberg, Henrik Oscarsson and Lena Wängnerud. Gothenburg: University of Gothenburg.
Palme, Joakim, et al. 2001. *Välfärdsbokslut för 1990-talet*. Stockholm: Fritzes Förlag.
Phillips, Anne. 1995. *The Politics of Presence*. Oxford: Oxford University Press.
Rönnbäck, Josefin. 2004. *Politikens Genusgränser. Den kvinnliga rösträttsrörelsen och kampen för kvinnors politiska medborgaskap 1902–1921*. Stockholm: Stockholm University.
Sainsbury, Diane. 1993. "The Politics of Increased Women's Representation: The Swedish Case." In *Gender and Party Politics*, ed. Joni Lovenduski and Pippa Norris. London: Sage.
Squires, Judith. 1999. *Gender and Political Theory*. Cambridge: Polity Press.
Teigen, Marie and Lena Wängnerud. 2009. "Tracing Gender Equality Cultures: Elite Perceptions in Norway and Sweden." *Politics & Gender* 5: 21–44.
Ulmanen, Petra. 1998. *(S)veket mot kvinnorna och hur högern stal feminismen*. Uddevalla: Atlas.
Verloo, Mieke. 2005. "Displacement and Empowerment: Reflections on the Concept and Practice of the Council of Europe Approach to Gender Mainstreaming and Gender Equality." *Social Politics* 12(3): 344–365.
Wängnerud, Lena. 2000a. "Testing the Politics of Presence: Women's Representation in the Swedish Riksdag." *Scandinavian Political Studies* 23(1): 67–91.
Wängnerud, Lena. 2000b. "Representing Women." In *Beyond Westminster and Congress: The Nordic Experience*, ed. Peter Esaiasson and Knut Heidar. Columbus: Ohio State University Press.
Wängnerud, Lena. 2001. "Kvinnors röst: En kamp mellan partier." In *Rösträtten 80 år. Forskarantologi*, ed. Christer Jönsson. Stockholm: Justitiedepartementet.

# 3 Gender-sensitive political representatives

"Women's interests" is a contested concept. Contemporary debates concern features of elitism in gender research – that is, a tendency to ascribe interests to women in a top-down fashion – and also features of essentialism: the tendency to view women and men as fixed, rather than changeable categories. Debates also concern how gender is related to categories such as ethnicity, age, and class (Dietz 2003). In her seminal book *The Concept of Representation* Hanna Pitkin (1967, 156) notes, however, that the concept of interests is "ubiquitous" in debates on representation. To differentiate interests is a matter of concretizing that which various groups can expect to gain through inclusion.

In this chapter we shall approach the question of *substantive representation* of women. Phillips (1995) presents reasons for expecting a link between descriptive and substantive representation. She states that there are "particular needs, interests, and concerns that arise from women's experience," and she continues, "these will be inadequately addressed in a politics dominated by men" (ibid., 66). To evaluate such statements, and test alternative explanations, we need a definition of "women's interests" that can be used in empirical analyses.

I share many of the doubts raised by feminist scholars regarding the usefulness of the concept of women's interests. The point of departure for this chapter is that interests are not set in stone, but formed in political debates and negotiations. Still, to follow developments in Sweden over time we need a starting point, and I believe that *self-determination* can be a starting point for a meaningful discussion on women's interests in contemporary societies.

Political parties can be described as collective entities with common ideology, programs, and strategies. Osborn (2012, 17) concludes that, "when women represent women, they do so as partisans." What Osborn (ibid.) stresses is that legislators are "nested" within political parties and that this limits the policies that women representatives can pursue. Equally important to note, however, is that parties change over time, and the recruitment of women can be seen as an endogenous factor affecting the agendas of political parties. Parties are made up of individuals, and at the same time as they can be described as collective entities, they can be described as arenas where different interests encounter each other. In this chapter the critical question is, *Do women and men have different interests?* If so, *Do female and male representatives champion those interests in different ways?* We should not expect a clear-cut "yes" or "no" answer – more interesting to note is variation across time and across political parties.

The chapter will proceed as follows: First, I shall discuss different approaches to the concept of women's interests and suggest a theoretical definition based on self-determination. Second, I shall anchor the theoretical definition of women's interests in the context of a Scandinavian welfare state and use empirical evidence from the SNES to validate the usefulness of a gendered approach to the concept of interests. The third step consists of an analysis of self-defined champions (Esaiasson 2000) of women's interests and concerns in the Riksdag. Together, these analyses will help us to identify gender-sensitive representatives.

Defining women's interests

In recent publications in the field of women, gender, and politics, it becomes obvious that researchers actively avoid substantive definitions of women's interests.[1] For example, Miki Caul Kittilson and Leslie A. Schwindt-Bayer state:

> We recognize that women are a diverse group that does not have an inherent, universal, or cohesive set of interests. We do suggest, however, that one commonality among women is their long history of marginalization from politics and this provides a basis for some women to organize and a base to which parties may seek electoral support.
> (ibid., 2012, 11)

Dahlerup and Leyenaar (2013, 217) discuss how a "difference discourse" can be forced upon women politicians and note that it may be a career liability to be identified as an advocate for women. Osborn (2012, 27) warns against normative assessments that obscure differences among women in the types of policy responsiveness they desire, and argues for an approach that stays within "feminist bounds" (ibid., 31).

What can be read between the lines in the books mentioned above is an acceptance of a minimalistic approach to women's interests; that is to say, it is in women's interests to be included in democratic processes. Other scholars stretch the boundaries and suggest some ideas for a specific content that is in line with women-friendly policies. In a study of legislative behavior in the United States (in the state legislatures of Arizona and California) Beth Reingold suggests that any definition of women's issues: (i) should delineate the primary subject matter of the questions or problems at hand (women); and (ii) give general (feminist) directions for answering these questions and solving the problems (Reingold 2000, 166). In her empirical analyses

Reingold (ibid.) connects women's issues to indicators such as advocacy of federally funded child care, concern about rape and domestic violence, and improvement of women's employment. A similar line of reasoning is found in Schwindt-Bayer's (2010) study on gender and politics in Latin America. Schwindt-Bayer founds her study on a definition of women's issues that emphasizes policies *liberalizing* reproductive rights and policies *equalizing* the civil rights of women and men in relation to areas such as education and employment.

Anne Phillips's line of reasoning has, in Chapter 1, been presented as a mainstream argumentation in research on women in politics. In a key quote she states:

> Women have distinct interests in relation to child-bearing (for any foreseeable future, an exclusively female affair); and as society is currently constituted they also have particular interests arising from their exposure to sexual harassment and violence, their unequal position in the division of paid and unpaid labor and their exclusion from most arenas of economic or political power.
> (ibid., 1995, 67–68)

Two things are comparatively uncontroversial in the quote above: First, the emphasis on marginalization (their exclusion from most arenas of economic and political power), and second, the emphasis on context (as society is currently constituted). The contextual approach implies that concepts such as women's interests and gender equality have to be anchored in time and space. A bit more controversial is the statement that women have distinct interests in relation to childbearing. However, similarly to Reingold (2000) and Schwindt-Bayer (2010), Phillips argues for policies strengthening the position of women vis-à-vis men.

Self-determination as a starting point

Few deny that gender-related differences such as childbearing exist in contemporary societies, but the connection to the political sphere is obviously disputed. I believe that a way forward is to divide the work of defining the concept of women's interests into several steps. A useful first step is to look at how the United Nations (UN) defines the concept of human development. In the *Global Human Development Report* (2006) the UN stresses capability aspects and says that human development has to do with the opportunity for people to realize their potential as human beings. The UN moves on to say that real opportunity is about having real choices – that is, choices that come with "a sufficient income, an education, good health and living in a country that is not governed by tyranny." Thus, the lack of a sufficient income and so forth can be seen as structures that may hinder people – women as well as men – from realizing their potential.

In *Multiculturalism Without Culture*, Anne Phillips (2007) presents a similar line of reasoning when she discusses how different cultures may curtail an individual's room to maneuver in society. Phillips portrays autonomy as worth striving for, and when she defines autonomy she points out the capability of people to make choices that, in some significant sense, are their own:

> I take autonomy as the capacity to reflect on and, within the limits of our circumstances, either endorse or change the way we act or live – thus, in some significant sense, to make our actions and choices our own.
> (ibid., 2007, 101)

For the purpose of this book it is important to note that Phillips suggests that self-determination is a matter of degrees, something of which individuals can have more or less (cf. Friedman 2000). Also important to note is that she brings forth an aspect of politicization. Phillips (2007, 127) assumes that societies will not achieve equality between women and men by simply disregarding gender-related differences. This assumption can be linked to Pitkin's (1967, 209) definition of representation, which is centered on acting: "Representation here means acting in the interest of the represented, in a manner responsive to them." As stated elsewhere in this book, for interests to get attention, someone needs to act.

I think most political scientists would agree that in gender-equal democracies, women and men are equally able to choose between political alternatives that address their specific concerns. This is a matter of having significant and meaningful choices. If self-determination is the starting point, what we should look for in the next step is gendered aspects of the ability to make significant and meaningful choices in a concrete context.

Self-determination in the context of a Scandinavian welfare state

What the UN suggests is a definition of human development that is applicable worldwide. Sweden is not "governed by tyranny," and gender equality, in the sense of formal equal rights, has been reached (see Chapter 6 of this book). Moreover, a conservative male-breadwinner model, where women's room to maneuver is limited to the private sphere, has been replaced by a dual-breadwinner model, where most women earn an income of their own (Melby et al. 2009; Sainsbury 1999). Thus, one needs to look for more subtle aspects of capability to capture lingering inequalities between women and men.

There are differences between Scandinavian countries, and changes occur over time; however, if one zooms out, there are some aspects of the Scandinavian welfare state that are necessary to point out in a discussion on the concept of women's interests.[2] The first thing to note is that women have made inroads into the political sphere, but in other arenas of power, especially the economic arena, are lagging behind.[3] In a report from 2013 the European

Commission states that Sweden is doing better than the European Union (EU) average: women represent 25.5 percent of the board members of the largest publicly listed companies in Sweden (EU average 15.8 percent), but only 3.8 percent of CEOs in Sweden are women. Estimates from Statistics Sweden show that women's economic assets are about 75 percent of men's economic assets (net worth). Moreover, women's wages are on average 16 percent lower than men's in terms of the entire labor market. If consideration is given to gender differences in occupation, education, age, and working hours, the difference is reduced to 6 percent.

The second thing to note is that Scandinavian welfare states have given rise to what is known as women's "double dependence" on the welfare state. In Sweden 82.5 percent of women and 88.7 percent of men aged 15–64 years are in the labor force (figures for 2011). However, on average, 32 percent of women compared to 10 percent of men work part time. Among women with young children, almost half work part time. Moreover, if we compare the private and the public sectors, striking differences appear: women constitute 39 percent of employees in the private sector, whereas the corresponding figure for the public sector is 74 percent. Occupations related to social work and personal care are dominant among women. This is not the place to get too far into details; the important conclusion is that Scandinavian welfare states contribute to economic independence for women, but they also produce a situation where broad layers of the female population are dependent on the welfare state, both as wage earners and as caregivers for children, elderly people, and other dependents.[4]

The third thing to note in a discussion about Scandinavian welfare states has to do with personal integrity. The Swedish Crime Survey shows that in Sweden, as in most other countries, young men form the group most likely to be subjected to assault. However, it is young women as a group who most strongly fear attack or assault. In all age groups, a higher proportion of women than men fear attack or assault, and reports show that when a woman is the victim a man most often is the perpetrator, whereas when a man is the victim another man most often is the perpetrator. It is notoriously hard to put the presence of threats, sexual harassment, and violence in a comparative perspective; the purpose of reporting these results from the Crime Survey is just to show that issues of personal integrity and safety have a gendered dimension in Sweden as well.

In sum, all definitions of women's interests will end up a bit simplified. However, I perceive this to be a risk worth taking. It is through this lens that we can start to ask the important issues in the field of representation: Whom do elected politicians represent? What is at stake in the parliamentary process? What is it, more exactly, that we can expect women to gain through inclusion in democratic processes? Women's room to maneuver in Sweden is different from men's. Women have fewer economic assets, and they are more vulnerable in the conflict between work and family. Women also, to a greater extent than men, adjust their way of living to avoid violence and crime. At the same time, it could be mentioned that more women than men in Sweden participate in higher education. Women are not discriminated against along all dimensions.

Most feminist scholars agree with Phillips's assumption that societies will not achieve equality between women and men by simply disregarding gender-related differences. Based on the previous discussion, I therefore suggest that women's interests can be narrowed down to three concerns: the recognition of women as a social category; the acknowledgment of the unequal balance of power between the sexes; and the occurrence of policies designed to increase the self-determination of female citizens. In the context of a Scandinavian welfare state the last aspect includes policies related to personal integrity and to the conflict between work and family, what Hege Skjeie (1992) has labeled care-and-career politics.

Validating the usefulness of a gendered approach to the concept of interests

We should remind ourselves that the theoretical definition of women's interests centers on self-determination and being able to choose between alternatives that address women's specific concerns. The theoretical definition does not put one type of solution before any other. A critique mentioned previously has to do with elitism – that is, a tendency to ascribe interests to women in a top-down fashion. Osborn (2012, 25) is sharp in her criticism of previous studies in the field of women, gender, and politics that begin with normative assumptions about women's interests and concerns:

> Therefore, studies of women legislators' representation of women examine whether women create policy outputs that benefit women according to these normative assumptions, but they do not consider whether women in society demand these actions.
>
> (Ibid.)

The point made is important: all theoretical definitions of women's interests need a "checkpoint." In this section I shall use data from SNES to validate the usefulness of a gendered approach to the concept of interests in contemporary Sweden.

Gender gaps related to political inclusion

So far, we have seen that a high number of women are elected to the Riksdag. Other indicators support the description that women in Sweden are included in democratic processes at the elite level of society. How does it look if we turn to the level of citizens? Data from the SNES show that gender gaps related to political inclusion have decreased in Sweden since the 1960s. For example, when it comes to turnout and party membership, there are currently no significant differences between male and female citizens

42 *Gender-sensitive political representatives*

(Oskarson and Wängnerud 2013). One area where there still is a gender gap, however, is citizens' subjective political interest.

Figure 3.1 reports findings on gender gaps in self-reported political interest, 1960–2010.

The first thing to note is that the level of political interest has increased in Sweden since the 1960s. What the results in Figure 3.1 visualize is that this increase is due to changes among women: in 1960 32 percent of women reported that they were very or fairly interested in politics; in 2010 the corresponding figure was 53 percent, which represents an increase of 21 percentage points. Among men, the level has remained rather stable: in 1960 57 percent of men reported that they were very or fairly interested in politics; in 2010 the corresponding figure was 59 percent. If we turn to changes in the size of the gender gap, the results in Figure 3.1 show that in 1960 the gender gap was 25 percentage points, but it was only 6 percentage points in 2010.

It is tempting to get into a discussion about explanations for the developments reported. The 1960s and 1970s was a period when the welfare state expanded in Sweden and women's involvement in higher education and the

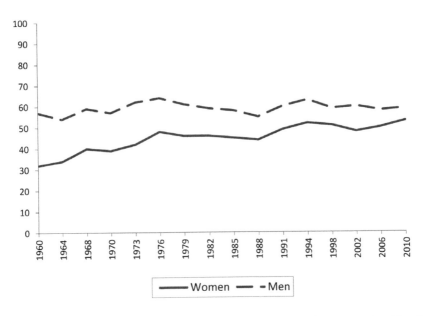

Figure 3.1 Political interest among women and men in Sweden, 1960–2010 (% of very and fairly interested)

Self-reported political interest. Respondents could choose between four response alternatives: "very interested," "fairly interested," "not so interested," or "not interested at all." The figure shows the merged categories very and fairly interested. Approximately 2,000–3,000 respondents on each occasion.

(Oskarson and Wängnerud 1995; additional data provided by Per Hedberg, SNES, Department of Political Science, University of Gothenburg)

paid labor force became much stronger. However, the important observation is that most indicators of political inclusion point in the same direction – toward a closing gender gap. Compared with earlier periods, current differences between women and men are small. In the next section we shall look at results for a number of indicators that are related to political content; these indicators do not, to the same extent, show a narrowing gender gap.

Gender gaps related to political content

Citizens' policy priorities and attitudes toward different policy alternatives are two indicators frequently used in studies on voting behavior and political representation.[5] Research on attitudes examines the solutions that are favored once an issue is on the political agenda. In contrast, research on priorities focuses on an earlier step, asking which issues receive attention in the first place.

If we think of the definition of women's interests launched previously, it should be most important to check priorities: are gender-related differences in citizens' everyday lives reflected in their perceptions of important policy areas? Measures of attitudes can also tell an interesting story. In this section, we shall look first at attitudes toward two proposals that relate to the structure of the welfare state: (i) a proposal to *reduce the public sector*; and (ii) a proposal to *provide more health care under private management*. Second, we shall look at two proposals that more clearly relate to the theoretical definition of women's interests: (iii) a proposal to *ban all forms of pornography*, which relates to personal integrity; and (iv) a proposal to *introduce a six-hour workday for all workers*, which relates to the possibility of successfully combining work and family.

Table 3.1 presents the results from an open-ended question in the SNES questionnaires. Respondents are asked to state what they consider the most important issues in deciding their choice of party. The answers are classified according to a detailed coding scheme. Table 3.1 reports the three most frequently mentioned policy areas among women and men, 1985–2010. The gray shading marks the policy area "social policy." For 2010 I have also included results for two broad categories: the first merging all respondents answering "social policy," "health care," or "elderly care"; and the second merging all respondents answering "jobs" or "the economy."

The results show that since the 1998 election women have identified social policy as the policy area most important in informing their decision about which party to vote for. The gray shading shows that, over time, social policy becomes one of the top three issues for men as well. However, it is only in the 2002 election that social policy is the most frequently mentioned area by men. High on men's lists we find jobs, taxes, and the economy. Women also frequently mentioned jobs as an important policy area, but not taxes or the economy.

44 *Gender-sensitive political representatives*

Table 3.1 The three most important policy areas in Swedish voters' choice of party, 1985–2010

	Women	%	Men	%
2010	Social policy	44	Jobs	33
	Education	33	Social policy	29
	Jobs	30	Economy	20
2006	Social policy	39	Jobs	37
	Jobs	32	Social policy	26
	Education	31	Education	18
2002	Social policy	54	Social policy	44
	Education	43	Education	35
	Pensions/elderly care	29	Taxes	25
1998	Social policy	30	Jobs	33
	Jobs	27	Social policy	20
	Pensions/elderly care	19	Taxes	18
1994	Jobs	39	Jobs	42
	Environment	26	Economy	37
	Social policy	25	Social policy	18
1991	Environment	29	Economy	24
	Social policy	27	Jobs	23
	Family policy	26	Environment	22
1988	Environment	50	Environment	43
	Family policy	24	Taxes	23
	Social policy	18	Social policy	12
1985	Family policy	25	Jobs	26
	Environment	23	Environment	23
	Jobs	23	Taxes	23

A special look at 2010

	Social policy/health care/elderly care	Jobs/economy
Women	54%	38%
Men	40%	48%
Diff.	+14	−10

(Oskarson and Wängnerud 1995; additional data provided by Per Hedberg, SNES, Department of Political Science, University of Gothenburg)

Results are based on an open-ended question in which respondents were permitted to choose any area or areas (more than one area could be mentioned). Approximately 2,000–3,000 respondents on each occasion.

The results for the merged categories in 2010 underline that there is a gender gap in attention paid to different policy areas. More women than men emphasized social policy, health care, and elderly care, and more men than women emphasized jobs and the economy. One can always dispute whether the gaps are small or large – whether the glass is half empty or half full – but I believe that the results underline the usefulness of a gendered approach to the concept of interests. A politics dominated by economy, taxes, and jobs does not reflect women's interests and concerns, and will not provide women with a sufficient basis for making significant and meaningful choices. This conclusion is further supported by the following analysis on gender gaps in attitudes.

Figure 3.2 shows attitudes toward four different policy alternatives that have featured in the political debate in Sweden. Dotted lines represent attitudes among men, and solid lines attitudes among women. Percentages represent the number who answered that it was a "very good" or "fairly good" proposal – that is, the numbers supporting each alternative.

I shall start by commenting on the fact that the two proposals measuring attitudes toward the structure of the welfare state, reductions in the public sector and provision of more health care under private management, display comparatively small gender gaps. For the proposal to reduce the public sector, the gender gap is actually decreasing over time. It is worth noting that attitudes among male citizens on this specific proposal are becoming more in line with the attitudes among female citizens, resulting in a rather low level of support. For the proposal to provide more health care under private management, the gender gap among citizens has never been big, and here also the results display a rather low level of support (there is a decrease in support over time). Thus, the main finding here is that when proposals concern the structure of the welfare state, we find small gender gaps among citizens in Sweden.

The next thing to comment on is that results look different when we focus on the two other proposals included in Figure 3.2: to ban all forms of pornography, and to introduce a six-hour workday for all workers. In an earlier section, I mentioned pornography as an issue that affects personal integrity for women and the introduction of a six-hour workday as an issue that affects the possibility for women to successfully combine work and family. The results in Figure 3.2 illustrate that the gender gaps are comparatively large regarding these two proposals, and it is worth noting that among female citizens, support for the proposals to ban all forms of pornography and to introduce a six-hour workday remained stable between 1985 and 2010: a majority of women support both of these proposals.

The analyses based on data from SNES confirm that gender is a significant factor in contemporary Swedish politics. In Sweden there seems to be little conflict between women and men on the structure of the welfare state – that is, issues pertaining to the size of the public sector and the

46 *Gender-sensitive political representatives*

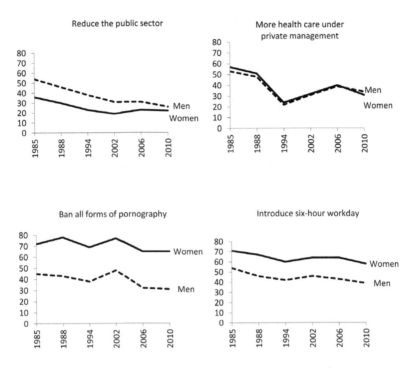

Figure 3.2 Proportion of voters in Sweden who support specific proposals, 1985–2010 (%)

The question reads: "The following list covers a number of proposals that have featured in the political debate. What is your opinion of each of them?" For each proposal, the alternatives were: "very good proposal," "good proposal," "neither good nor bad proposal," "bad proposal," and "very bad proposal." The figure shows the percentage in favor ("very good" and "good" combined). The exact wording of each proposal: "reduce the public sector," "provide more health care under private management," "ban all forms of pornography," and "introduce a six-hour workday for all workers." There were approximately 2,000–3,000 respondents on each occasion.(Oskarson and Wängnerud 1995; additional data provided by Per Hedberg, SNES, Department of Political Science, University of Gothenburg)

element of private management. Where female and male citizens differ is in the emphasis on social policy and on standpoints pertaining to personal integrity and the possibility of successfully combining work and family.

Self-defined champions of women's interests

In this chapter we have begun to approach the question of substantive representation of women, that is, the effect of women's presence in parliament, and the whole point of this book is that we cannot take this effect for granted. On the one hand, presence theories provide reasons for expecting a link between descriptive and substantive representation. On the other hand, theories on group awareness provide reasons for expecting effects of the intentional representation of different social groups. Theories on group awareness do not ascribe importance to women politicians per se, but to politicians who are sensitive to social group experiences and "the history of social group relations" (Young 2000, 134).

The final answer to the question of substantive representation will not be reached until the end of this book. In this section we shall answer the question, *Do women and men representatives champion women's interests in different ways?*

As early as the beginning of the 1990s Hege Skjeie (1992) was arguing that the growing presence of female politicians in Norway had made male politicians in the Norwegian national parliament, the Stortinget, more supportive of women's interests and concerns. In a similar line of reasoning, Dahlerup (2006, 518) warns against a "difference fallacy" and highlights "the obvious possibility that women, as politicians, perhaps especially when there are many of them, have been able to influence their male colleagues and thus change either the overall political agenda or the agenda of their individual parties." These assumptions can be summarized in the expectation of a spillover effect.

It is an empirical question of whether self-defined champions of women's interests – that is, those who single out women as an important group to represent – act in a manner different from their colleagues. Previous research (Esaiasson 2000) shows an effect, but few observers have been able to follow developments over a longer period of time. Before we move on to the other chapters of this book, we need to know what changes are occurring in the Riksdag. Do more women in parliament mean a higher proportion of self-defined champions of women's interests?

Dynamic explanatory themes

We need to look at research on opinion-formation processes among citizens to get a more thorough understanding of dynamic explanatory themes: what changes is it reasonable to expect? Bolzendahl and Myers (2004) discuss opinion-formation processes in relation to support for feminism and gender equality. They make a useful distinction between interest-based and exposure-based approaches. The fundamental concept in exposure-based approaches is that individuals develop or change their understandings of women's place in society when they encounter ideas and experiences that resonate with feminist ideals (ibid.). The effect can be expected to be particularly strong among men, as they often lack women's feminist awareness and experiences. Bolzendahl and Myers's focus is on how encounters with feminist ideas and experiences in the family, educational settings, and workplaces affect individuals' attitudes, but their analysis should reasonably apply to political settings as well (Kokkonen and Wängnerud 2014).

The idea that the attitudes and beliefs that surround us affect our own attitudes and beliefs is by now well established in social psychology. Social comparison theory, for example, suggests that people often assess the correctness of their views by comparing them with the views held by people around them (e.g. Festinger 1950; Visser and Mirabile 2004). Group conformity tends to generate social rewards, such as acceptance and approval, whereas divergence from group norms often results in social sanctions, such as rejection and derogation. Research has also shown that "publicly expressing one's views and otherwise behaviourally committing to them renders attitudes stronger" (Visser and Mirabile 2004, 81). Mechanisms such as these strongly suggest that the benefits of expressing feminist attitudes and the costs of expressing non-feminist attitudes will increase as more women enter politics (Kokkonen and Wängnerud 2014).

There are, however, also theoretical reasons for assuming a null effect on male politicians' views. Feminist institutionalism points out that institutions such as parliaments are gendered, and thereby provide informal rules about appropriate gendered behavior (Chappell and Waylen 2013; Hawkesworth 2005; Krook and Mackay 2010). Along this line of reasoning one can expect distinct roles for male and female politicians, and a situation where female politicians are assigned the role as the most fervent champions of women's interests and concerns.

A third explanatory theme has to do with period-specific events. In voter studies researchers distinguish between cohort effects and aging effects. The theoretical idea behind aging effects is that life experiences matter for political attitudes and behavior, whereas the theoretical idea behind cohort effects is that, all things being equal, persons who became politically active during a certain period bear some remnants of that period. A much-used example is cohorts of Americans who were socialized before Roosevelt's New Deal of the 1930s, who have been shown to be more Republican than other comparable cohorts (see Tilley 2002, 122).

Studies on cohort effects are relatively rare in research on political representatives. An important exception is Barbara Sinclair's (1989) research on the transformations of the US Senate. The point of departure of her study is a change in American politics. In the 1950s the US Senate was an "encapsulated men's club," out of touch with citizens. Sinclair notes a transformation toward an outward-looking institution with more room to maneuver for individual politicians. She contends that an important factor behind this change was pressure exerted by liberal northern Democrats who entered the US Senate in large numbers in the early 1960s. For the advancement of this study it is important to note that the influx of liberal northern Democrats into the US Senate was accompanied by the emergence of new issues in American politics, such as those concerning the Vietnam War and the Civil Rights Movement. Sinclair argues that the transformation of the US Senate was driven by two distinct processes: the influx of large numbers of newcomers, and a major change in the issue agenda. The latter process originated in the external environment (i.e., outside the US Senate), with pressure groups and social movements, often in accordance with the media, driving that change (Sinclair 1989, 67).

A question for this book is whether the 1994 Swedish election resulted in a similar change in the Riksdag. In that election the Support Stockings network, often in accordance with the media, put pressure on the established political parties regarding feminism and gender equality (see Chapter 2 in this book). Moreover, turnover in the Riksdag was especially high in that election. Analyses (Ahlbäck Öberg et al. 2007) demonstrate that during the 1970s and 1980s the situation was quite stable in the Swedish parliament; in every election there was a turnover of about 20 percent of the seats. Then in the 1991 election something happened. Suddenly there was a turnover of about 30 percent of the seats, and in the 1994 election the turnover increased to more than 35 percent.[6]

It should not be taken for granted that more women in parliament means a higher proportion of self-defined champions of women's interests. Exposure-based theories underpin the notion of a spillover effect, which should result in a higher proportion of male politicians who are sensitive to women's interests and concerns. Feminist institutionalism, however, gives reason to expect a null effect on male politicians' views, and research based on time-specific events foresees "bumps" – that is, strengthened support for women's interests and concerns during certain periods, and waning support in between.

MPs' personal commitment to women as a group

What is a self-defined champion of women's interests? The question used in the forthcoming analyses concerns how important it is to MPs, personally, to promote different groups in society. The question includes items that relate not only to the party, the constituency, and individual voters, but also to groups such as businesspeople, farmers, women, and wage earners. The forthcoming analyses single out how important it is to MPs personally to promote women's interests and concerns. Self-defined champions of women's interests are assumed to believe that it is *very important* to promote women's interests and concerns. Figure 3.3 shows the proportion of Swedish MPs who answered that it was "very important" to promote women's interests and concerns, in 1985–2010.

The overall impression of the results reported in Figure 3.3 is stability. In 1985 24 percent of all Swedish MPs can be classified as self-defined champions of women's interests. The corresponding figure for 2010 is 28 percent. The most noticeable change in Figure 3.3 is the drop in the self-perceived importance among women of promoting women's interests in the Riksdag, from 55 percent in 1985 to 45 percent in 2010, and the increase among men from 10 percent in 1985 to 16 percent in 2010.

50 *Gender-sensitive political representatives*

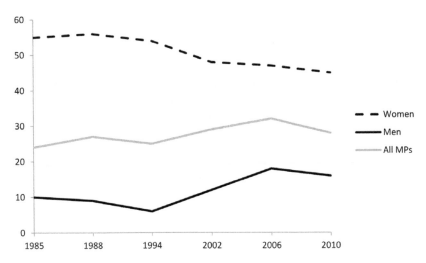

Figure 3.3 Proportion of Swedish MPs who answered that it was "very important" to promote women's interests and concerns, 1985–2010 (%)
The question reads, "How important are the following tasks to you personally as a member of parliament?" The MPs were asked to rank about ten representative tasks, such as "promote your party's policies" and "promote your region's/constituency's interests and concerns." The following response alternatives were offered: "very important," "fairly important," "fairly unimportant," and "not at all important."
(Swedish Parliamentary Surveys, Department of Political Science, University of Gothenburg)

The increase among men may be related to a spillover effect. Based on previous research, however, it is hard to explain the drop among women in the Riksdag. In the next step we shall turn to a multivariate regression analysis to capture variations across time and across different groups of MPs. The analysis in Table 3.2 focuses on 1988, 1994, and 2010, and in addition to MPs' gender and party affiliation, the analysis includes age, parliamentary experience, and education, and whether the MPs hold a distinguished power position such as being a chair of a standing committee, a member of the party board, or similar.

There are several things to note in Table 3.2. First of all, it comes as no surprise that there is a significant effect of gender in all analyses: Even though there is a downward trend among women (Figure 3.3), female MPs are on all survey occasions the most fervent representatives of women's interests and concerns. Second, the results in Table 3.2 show no significant effect of age (the variable captures respondents' age in years), but in 1994 there is a significant effect of parliamentary experience, which means that newly elected MPs were more inclined than their senior colleagues to answer that it is "very important" to promote women's interests and concerns.

A third thing to note in Table 3.2 is that results for the effect of party affiliation show that all the parties included are significantly different from

Table 3.2 Determinants of Swedish MPs' commitment to represent women's issues and concerns 1988, 1994, and 2010 (logistic regression)

	1988			1994			2010		
	B	SE	Sig.	B	SE	Sig.	B	SE	Sig.
Gender	2.64	0.39	0.00	3.44	0.46	0.00	1.45	0.31	0.00
Lft	2.65	0.98	0.00	3.88	0.95	0.00	2.11	0.63	0.00
SocDem	0.95	0.62	0.12	2.14	0.73	0.00	0.70	0.40	0.08
Grn	–	–	–	2.66	1.01	0.00	0.76	0.58	0.19
Cen	1.02	0.71	0.15	3.01	0.92	0.00	-0.36	0.84	0.66
Lib	0.21	0.74	0.77	3.63	0.91	0.00	0.09	0.67	0.88
ChrDem	n.a.	n.a.	n.a.	2.36	1.15	0.04	-0.71	0.83	0.38
SweDem	n.a.	n.a.	n.a.	n.a.	n.a.	n.a.	–	–	–
Con (reference)									
Age	0.02	0.03	0.46	0.03	0.02	0.11	0.00	0.01	0.66
Experience	-0.03	0.04	0.37	-0.10	0.04	0.01	0.00	0.03	0.80
Education	-0.25	0.38	0.51	0.02	0.38	0.95	-0.07	0.36	0.83
Power position	0.06	0.42	0.88	-1.58	0.48	0.00	-0.91	0.38	0.01
Constant	-3.93	1.64	0.01	-6.30	1.54	0.00	-2.07	0.89	0.02
Nagelkerke	0.38			0.55			0.26		

(Swedish Parliamentary Surveys, Department of Political Science, University of Gothenburg)

See Figure 3.3 for information on the question asked. See the Appendices for information on the different categories.

the Conservative Party in 1994, but not on the other survey occasions. In 2010 it is only the results for the Left Party and the Social Democratic Party that are significantly different from the Conservative Party. The final thing to note in Table 3.2 is that the variable "power position" is significant in 1994 and 2010: the results show that MPs holding a distinguishable power position are less inclined than others to single out women as an important group.

Before concluding this chapter, let us take a closer look at the effect of various periods. The 1994 election, with its "window of opportunity" (Teigen and Wängnerud 2009) for radical feminism, was different from previous elections in Sweden. Figure 3.4 presents a cohort analysis in which it is possible to follow newcomers in the Riksdag over four terms (Öhberg and Wängnerud 2014). The results should be read as responses to these questions: Among, for example, newcomers in the 1985 election, how many were self-defined champions of women's interests? What is the corresponding figure when this group starts their second, third, and fourth terms in parliament? I stop after four terms, as the number of individuals in each cohort shrinks over time; only a handful of politicians hold a seat in the Riksdag for more than four terms.

The results in Figure 3.4 show that newcomers in the 1994 election start at a high level in terms of being self-defined champions of women's interests: 45 percent answered that it is very important to them personally to promote women's interests and concerns. There is a drop in the 1994 cohort between their first and second terms; however, compared with other cohorts of newcomers, they remain at a high level. Unfortunately, there are no data regarding the first term in parliament for the newcomers in the 1991 election. However, it is reasonable to conclude that newcomers in the 1991 election and newcomers in the 1994 election are contrasting cases; measured this way, the cohort of 1994 stands out as the most gender-sensitive generation in the Swedish Riksdag, whereas the newcomers in the 1991 election stand out as the least gender-sensitive generation.

Öhberg and Wängnerud (2014) report results from a panel analysis in which the cohort of 1994 is compared with all the other Swedish parliamentarians between the years 1985 and 2010. Their results confirm that the cohort of 1994 was more inclined to promote women's issues and concerns compared with other generations, and most importantly, there is an effect that remains significant when controlling for gender.[7]

Additional analyses confirm that how MPs perceive the task of promoting women's interests and concerns is correlated to MPs' positions on the left–right scale, but most interesting in these additional analyses is the fact that the result for the cohort of 1994 is not driven only by the left-leaning newcomers. Actually, more than one third (36 percent) of the newcomers from parties to the right could be categorized as self-defined champions of women's interests in the 1994 election. This is in clear contrast to their senior colleagues, of whom only slightly over one tenth (12 percent) answered that it was

Gender-sensitive political representatives 53

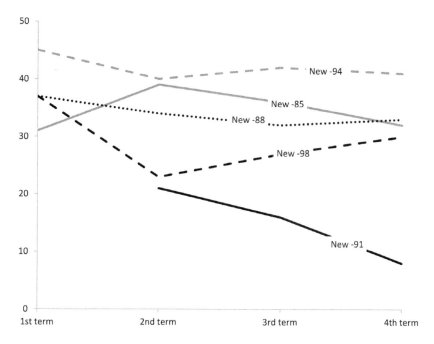

Figure 3.4 The development of newly elected MPs' commitment to women's issues and concerns over four terms (%)

The results show percentages answering that it is "very important" to promote women's interests and concerns (see Figure 3.3 for details). Note that there was no Parliamentary Survey in 1991, which means that the value "3rd" term for "New −85" represents a mean between the values for the 2nd and 4th terms, and, correspondingly, the value "2nd term" for "New −88" represents a mean between the values for the 1st and 3rd terms. It also means that there are no data for "New −91" on their first term in parliament.
(Öhberg and Wängnerud 2014; data from Parliamentary Surveys, Department of Political Science, University of Gothenburg)

very important to them personally to promote women's interests and concerns (Öhberg and Wängnerud 2013).

These analyses underpin the notion that one cannot take for granted that more women in parliament means a higher proportion of self-defined champions of women's interests. Overall, the proportion of self-defined champions of women's interests remained remarkably stable between 1985 and 2010 (during this period the proportion of women in the Riksdag increased from 32 to 45 percent). However, *who* these self-defined champions are varies over time. In 1994 self-defined champions can, more or less, be found throughout the Riksdag, and especially among newcomers, but in 2010 the results are structured not only by the gender dimension but also the ideological left–right dimension.

Can we expect effects of being a self-defined champion?

Not all female politicians are self-defined champions of women's interests, and some male politicians are. The results presented in this section indicate that it may be important to separate presence theories from theories on group awareness. Chapter 2 included an analysis of MPs' attitudes toward different arguments for why there should be equal distribution of women and men in parliament. One argument, that there will be consequences for policies, was linked to ideas and strategies of reversal. The last empirical analysis in this chapter is a cross-tabulation between the question of how important MPs think it is, to them personally, to promote women's interests and concerns, and the question of how important they think the argument is that "there will be consequences for policies." The gray shading in Table 3.3 shows the percentages who answered that promoting women's interests and concerns is very important to them personally *and* that the argument that there will be consequences for policies is very important.

The results in Table 3.3 show that among women these two things largely coincide: a majority among women MPs who think it is very important to promote women's interests and concerns also support the idea that there will be consequences for policies. The overlap is smaller among male politicians: 25 percent in 1994 and 30 percent in 2010 are found in the category where the two indicators coincide.

Being a gender-sensitive representative

The concept of women's interests is contested. This book spans a period of 25 years; some analyses cover even longer periods. In such a perspective major changes take place in society, and the definition given previously may in the end turn out to be too static.[8] The aim of this chapter has been twofold: to answer the question of whether women and men have different interests, and, if so, whether female and male representatives champion those interests in different ways. The answers to these questions were supposed to help us to understand what it means to be a gender-sensitive representative.

The concept of self-determination has been used as a starting point in the discussion of how theoretically to define women's interests. It is important to bear in mind that the core aspects brought forward have to do with the capability to make significant and meaningful choices. Interests are not set in stone but formed in political debates and negotiations. However, debates and negotiations that completely overlook real, everyday life experiences will be esoteric and of no use in transformative processes.

Many feminist scholars want to restrict the definition of women's interests to matters of inclusion in democratic processes. Even in 1991 Anna G. Jónasdóttir argued that the core element in the debate concerned *form*, being where authoritative decision making takes place. However, as gender gaps in political participation – both at the elite level of society and among citizens – decrease, the question of political *content* becomes ever more intrusive.

Table 3.3 Self-defined champions of women's interests and how they perceive the argument that there will be consequences for policies (%)

	Represent women's issues and concerns			
	1994		2010	
Consequences for policies	Very important	Fairly important/ not important	Very important	Fairly important/ not important
Women MPs				
Very important	65	33	54	29
Fairly important/not important	35	67	46	71
Sum	100	100	100	100
Men MPs				
Very important	25	7	30	13
Fairly important/not important	75	93	70	87
Sum	100	100	100	100
All MPs				
Very important	59	13	46	18
Fairly important/not important	41	87	54	82
Sum	100	100	100	100

(Swedish Parliamentary Surveys, Department of Political Science, University of Gothenburg)

The table reports results of a cross-tabulation of responses to two questions: (i) "How important are the following tasks to you personally as a member of parliament?" Included here are responses to the task "promote women's issues and concerns." The following response alternatives were offered: "very important," "fairly important," "fairly unimportant," and "not at all important." In the table the categories "fairly important," "fairly unimportant," and "not at all important" are merged. (ii) "There are various ways to argue for an equal distribution of women and men in the Riksdag. How important do you consider the following argument to be? There will be consequences for policies." The following response alternatives were offered: "very important," "fairly important," "not very important," and "not at all important." In the table the categories "fairly important," "not very important," and "not at all important" are merged.

The empirical analyses built on data from the SNES show that there are significant gender gaps among citizens in contemporary Sweden when it comes to policy priorities and attitudes. These results should be interpreted as a validation of the usefulness of a gendered approach to the concept of interest. Against this backdrop I suggested that the concept of women's interests should be narrowed down to three concerns: the recognition of women as a social category, the acknowledgment of the unequal balance of power between the sexes, and the occurrence of policies designed to increase the self-determination of female citizens. Taking into account the context of a

Scandinavian welfare state, the last aspect was said to include policies related to personal integrity and to the conflict between work and family.

The second part of this chapter has dealt with the first concern of the definition above: the recognition of women as a social category. It is not far-fetched to believe that elected representatives who say that it is very important to them personally to promote women's interests and concerns are more inclined than others to act in the interests of women. Forthcoming analyses will show whether this assumption holds. At this stage, however, I suggest a preliminary definition of a gender-sensitive representative as being tantamount to a self-defined champion of women's interests and concerns.

A final theme to touch upon before we move on to the next chapter in this book is that the spillover effect on male politicians' views is smaller than what might have been expected from previous research (Dahlerup 2006; Skjeie 1992). The results in this chapter put a question mark over expectations of a "smooth" process toward a gender-sensitive parliament. The results indicate a potential conflict between self-defined champions of women's interests and others. It should also be noted that female self-defined champions of women's interests seem to be "on top" in processes related to gender equality: they combine their personal commitment to women as a group with a belief that more women in parliament will have consequences for policy.

Notes

1 The debate on women's interests has a long history. The edited volume *Feminism and Politics* (Phillips 1998) serves as a good introduction.
2 See Bergqvist *et al.* (2000) for a thorough discussion on differences between Scandinavian/Nordic countries.
3 The figures in this and the next two sections build on official statistics published by Statistics Sweden on their website (www.scb.se), and summarized in the report *Women and Men in Sweden: Facts and Figures*. Figures refer to the latest available data.
4 It should also be noted that transfer systems connected to the welfare state, such as parental leave allowance, contribute to reduce gender gaps in disposable income.
5 For studies on political representation in Nordic countries, see Esaiasson and Heidar 2000.
6 In 1994 the parliamentary term was changed to four years instead of three, which contributed to the increase in turnover. In 1991 turnover was to a large extent explained by changes in voter support for different parties. In 1994 turnover caused by voters was comparatively low, but turnover due to other reasons reached an all-time high (Ahlbäck Öberg *et al.* 2007).
7 The cohort of 1994 had a 6-percentage-point higher probability of being a self-defined champion of women's interests than other generations. Moreover, the panel analysis confirms that being a self-defined champion of women's interests is related to being female and also to being a member of the Left Party. There is, however, no evidence of a link to any broader value change in society; when controlling for election year, there are no differences between time points. Öhberg and Wängnerud (2014) conducted controls for the backgrounds of the cohort of 1994. There is, for example, nothing in terms of socioeconomic factors that

distinguishes them from their senior colleagues, except for the fact that they are younger and more of them are women. In no other respect did the newcomers in that specific election represent a "new" kind of politician.

8 One thing to note is that the number of foreign-born residents has increased significantly during recent decades; these now make up about 15 percent of the Swedish population. About 25 percent of the Swedish population is either foreign-born or have at least one parent who was foreign-born. This makes the concept of women's interests even more problematic.

Bibliography

Ahlbäck Öberg, Shirin, Jörgen Hermansson and Lena Wängnerud. 2007. *Exit riksdagen*. Malmö: Liber.

Bergqvist, Christina, Anette Borchost, Ann-Dorte Christensen, Viveca Ramstedt-Silén, Nina C. Rauum and Auður Styrkársdóttir. 2000. *Equal Democracies? Gender and Politics in the Nordic Countries*. Oslo: Norwegian University Press.

Bolzendahl, Catherine I. and Daniel J. Myers. 2004. "Feminist Attitudes and Support for Gender Equality: Opinion Change in Women and Men, 1974–1998." *Social Forces* 83: 759–789.

Chappell, Louise and Georgina Waylen. 2013. "Gender and the Hidden Life of Institutions." *Public Administration* 91(3): 599–615.

Dahlerup, Drude. 2006. "The Story of the Theory of Critical Mass." *Politics & Gender* 2(4): 511–522.

Dahlerup, Drude and Monique Leyenaar, eds. 2013. *Breaking Male Dominance in Old Democracies*, Oxford: Oxford University Press.

Dietz, Mary G.. 2003. "Current Controversies in Feminist Theory." *Annual Review of Political Science* 6(1): 399–431.

Esaiasson, Peter. 2000. "How Members of Parliament Define their Task." In *Beyond Westminster and Congress: The Nordic Experience*, ed. Peter Esaiasson and Knut Heidar. Columbus: Ohio State University Press.

Esaiasson, Peter and Knut Heidar, eds. 2000. *Beyond Westminster and Congress: The Nordic Experience*. Columbus: Ohio State University Press.

Festinger, Leon. 1950. "Informal Social Communication." *Psychological Review* 57: 271–282.

Friedman, Marilyn. 2000. "Autonomy, Social Disruption, and Women." In *Relational Autonomy: Feminist Perspectives on Autonomy, Agency, and the Social Self*, ed. Catriona MacKenzie and Natalie Stoljar. Oxford: Oxford University Press.

Hawkesworth, Mary. 2005. "Engendering Political Science: An Immodest Proposal." *Politics & Gender* 1: 141–156.

Jónasdóttir, Anna G.. 1991. *Love Power and Political Interests: Towards a Theory of Patriarchy in Contemporary Western Societies*. Örebro Studies 7. Örebro: University of Örebro.

Kittilson, Miki Caul and Leslie A. Schwindt-Bayer. 2012. *The Gendered Effects of Electoral Institutions: Political Engagement and Participation*. Oxford: Oxford University Press.

Kokkonen, Andrej and Lena Wängnerud. 2014. *Women's Presence in Politics and Male Politicians Attitudes Toward Gender Equality in Politics*. Accepted for publication in *Journal of Women, Politics, and Policy*.

Krook, Mona Lena and Fiona Mackay, eds. 2010. *Gender, Politics and Institutions: Towards a Feminist Intuitionalism*. Basingstoke and New York: Palgrave Macmillan.
Melby, Kari, Anna-Birte Ravn and Christina Carlsson Wetterberg, eds. 2009. *Gender Equality and Welfare Politics in Scandinavia: The Limits of Political Ambition?* Bristol: The Policy Press.
Öhberg, Patrik and Lena Wängnerud. 2014. "Testing the Impact of Political Generations: The Class of 94 and Pro-feminist Ideas in the Swedish Riksdag." *Scandinavian Political Studies* 37(6): 61–81.
Osborn, Tracy L. 2012. *How Women Represent Women: Political Parties, Gender, and Representation in State Legislatures*. Oxford: Oxford University Press.
Oskarson, Maria and Lena Wängnerud. 1995. *Kvinnor som väljare och valda. Om betydelsen av kön i svensk politik*. Lund: Studentlitteratur.
Oskarson, Maria and Lena Wängnerud. 2013. "The Story of the Gender Gap in Swedish Politics: Only Partially Diminishing Differences." In *Stepping Stones: Research on Political Representation, Voting Behavior, and Quality of Government*, ed. Stefan Dahlberg, Henrik Oscarsson and Lena Wängnerud. Gothenburg: University of Gothenburg.
Phillips, Anne. 1995. *The Politics of Presence*. Oxford: Oxford University Press.
Phillips, Anne, ed. 1998. *Feminism and Politics*. Oxford: Oxford University Press.
Phillips, Anne. 2007. *Multiculturalism Without Culture*. Princeton, NJ: Princeton University Press.
Pitkin, Hanna F.. 1967. *The Concept of Representation*. Berkeley: University of California Press.
Reingold, Beth. 2000. *Representing Women: Sex, Gender, and Legislative Behavior in Arizona and California*. Chapel Hill: University of North Carolina Press.
Sainsbury, Diane, ed. 1999. *Gender and Welfare State Regimes*, Oxford: Oxford University Press.
Schwindt-Bayer, Leslie A. 2010. *Political Power and Women's Representation in Latin America*. Oxford: Oxford University Press.
Sinclair, Barbara. 1989. *The Transformation of the U.S. Senate*. Baltimore, MD: The Johns Hopkins University Press.
Skjeie, Hege. 1992. *Den politiske betydningen av kjønn. En studie av norsk topp-politikk*, rapport 92:11. Oslo: Inst. Samfunnsforskning.
Teigen, Marie and Lena Wängnerud. 2009. "Tracing Gender Equality Cultures: Elite Perceptions in Norway and Sweden." *Politics & Gender* 5: 21–44.
Tilley, James. 2002. "Political Generations and Partisanship in the UK, 1964–1997." *Journal of the Royal Statistical Society* 165(1): 121–135.
United Nations. 2006. *Global Human Development Report*. Available at: hdr.undp.org/en/content/human-development-report-2006.
Visser, Penny S. and Robert R. Mirabile. 2004. "Attitudes in the Social Context: The Impact of Social Network Composition on Individual-level Attitude Strength." *Journal of Personality and Social Psychology* 87(6): 779–795.
Young, Iris Marion. 2000. *Inclusion and Democracy*. Oxford: Oxford University Press.

4 Internal parliamentary working procedures

The 1994 election saw a breakthrough for women in Swedish politics: the proportion of women in the Riksdag passed the threshold of 40 percent; the number of women appointed cabinet minister was for the first time 50 percent; and, as shown in Chapter 3, there was a strong commitment to women's interests and concerns among newcomers to the Riksdag.

However, at the end of the parliamentary term, right before the 1998 election, the speaker of the parliament noted that a high proportion of young female MPs had chosen not to stand again. The speaker, Birgitta Dahl, a female Social Democrat, was worried, and initiated a research project on turnover. She wanted to know what the Riksdag, as an institution, could do to make young MPs stay. I was part of that project, and we found that young women were critical of their time in parliament. One woman said, "In the Riksdag, we do not discuss politics … we just meet and everything is so decided beforehand." She ended with the words: "I cannot stand that stuff, I think" (Ahlbäck Öberg et al. 2007, 100).

The woman quoted above represented the Left Party, and the quote illustrates the main finding of this chapter: women are more critical than men of their working conditions, and such criticism is especially pertinent in parties within the left-green bloc. However, this chapter will show that in most cases there is not much the speaker can do about it. It is the political parties that determine the everyday lives of elected representatives; the criticism women have is mainly of the party groups and less often of parliament as such.

This chapter focuses on *internal parliamentary working procedures*. The core question concerns whether women entering the Swedish parliament meet gender-specific obstacles and, if so, how great those obstacles are. The chapter is divided into two parts: First we shall look at indicators of formal power positions, such as being a standing committee member or board chair. Patterns of functional division – sometimes referred to as horizontal sex segregation – between women and men are mapped out and evaluated. In the second part we shall look at indicators of informal power, such as how female and male politicians perceive their own ability to make an impact. The chapter will start, though, with an overview of the debate on the individual versus institutional level of analysis in research on women, gender, and politics.

Old puzzle, new direction

The book *Unfinished Democracy: Women in Nordic Politics* was published in 1983 (Haavio-Mannila et al. 1983). This was the first comprehensive study on women's political participation in Nordic countries. The number of women in Nordic parliaments had started to increase but the advancement was not visible across all areas. Haavio-Mannila and colleagues (ibid.) distinguish two kinds of division between women and men in elected assemblies: those related to formal power, which they call hierarchical gender structures, and those related to policy areas, which they label functional gender structures.

Sue Thomas (1994) is a pioneer of empirical research on gender and committee assignments. In an analysis of state legislators in the United States, she follows developments over time. In the 1970s women representatives were concentrated in a very narrow set of committees, most often education committees; however, in the 1980s women were found in all kinds of committees, although the proportion of women and men was not equal on all types of committees. A 1988 survey showed that women were significantly more likely than men to be assigned to health and welfare committees; women were also less likely than men to sit on committees dealing with business and private economic concerns (Thomas 1994, 66).

Thomas also investigates the extent to which committee assignments reflect priorities among male and female politicians. Her conclusion from the 1988 survey was that gender patterns resulted from legislators' choices rather than coercion or discrimination (Thomas 1994, 67). A number of studies from different settings support this conclusion. Based on her study on state legislatures in Arizona and California, Reingold (2000, 179) states that "All told, the evidence suggests that whatever sex segregation in policy activity there was in these two legislatures was voluntary." Based on their study on assignments to political committees in Danish local politics, Martin Bækgaard and Ulrik Kjær (2012, 479) state that "Women and men sit in different committees primarily because they have different preferences." The suggestion has been made that women entering legislative bodies act strategically and take control over policy areas that affect broad layers of the female population (Skjeie 1992). The opposite interpretation is, however, also present in the literature: based on their study of women's representation on committees in Latin American legislatures, Roseanna Heath, Leslie Schwindt-Bayer, and Michelle Taylor-Robinson (2005) suggest that women are found on the "sidelines" of the political arena.

Feminist institutionalism

The increased influence of an institutional approach in research on women, gender, and politics has made the issue of choice versus coercion partly outdated. One particularly interesting example of feminist institutionalism can be found in Catherine Bolzendahl's (2014) study on the gendered organization of legislative committees in Germany, Sweden, and the United States. Taking a time perspective of 40 years, she theorizes the role of legislatures as gendered institutions that build gender into their institutional operation. Her main finding is a combination of stereotyping and organizational redesign that works to protect masculine privilege. Bolzendahl (2014, 2) contends that her "institutional-level approach suggests limitations to overly emphasizing individual-level processes, such as women's background, preferences and, interaction styles." The point made is that individual-level approaches are "neglecting constructions of masculinity" (ibid.). A similar line of reasoning is found in *Feminizing Politics* by Joni Lovenduski (2005), in which she argues that the most difficult obstacle female politicians meet is the deeply embedded culture of masculinity in political institutions (see also Kathlene 1994; Krook and Mackay 2010; and references within Bolzendahl 2014).

The core argument in this strand of research is that gender operates beyond the individual level and can be seen as an institution in itself. The questions raised are admittedly multilayered, but taken together, the most important assumption in feminist institutionalism is that legislators enter political organizations that are not gender neutral but have been created to maintain and reflect male dominance. Thus, the roles that women and men are able to play within legislatures are, at least partially, predetermined.

Feminist institutionalism is open to the fact that change may occur. In her comparison of Germany, Sweden, and the United States, Bolzendahl (2014) notices that the United States – she studies the US House of Representatives – comes closest to a masculine dominance gendered organization. In Germany the Bundestag is characterized as a polarized gendered organization whereas in Sweden the Riksdag is characterized as an egalitarian-trending gendered organization. In Sweden women increasingly sit on all committees and act as chair or vice-chair. Bolzendahl notes that Sweden's turn toward convergence came after many years of high levels of women's representation. She also notes that the Swedish system "simultaneously validates and institutionalizes social and familial issues as legitimate political affairs," which makes Sweden a distinctive case. Bolzendahl questions whether a similar pattern – convergence – would be found in Germany or the United States if levels of gender parity were similar (Bolzendahl 2014, 23).

I agree that it is problematic to overly emphasize individual-level processes. In this book I suggest an approach that moves back and forth between the level of parliaments as institutions, the level of political parties, and the level of individual politicians. At a minimum preferences expressed in surveys and interviews can help to inform interpretations of patterns that appear in data such as committee assignments. One area of contention is to what extent convergence is a driving force behind a gender-sensitive parliament. When Dahlerup and Leyenaar (2013, 302) identify gender balance in politics, two of the most important factors are: (i) that all leadership positions in elected assemblies and all positions in governments are equally (40–60) divided among men and women; and (ii) that a real state of gender neutrality is prevalent whereby portfolios are assigned without gender bias. The forthcoming analyses will, however, show that convergence in committee assignments in the Riksdag has not led to disappeared or reduced gender gaps in dissatisfaction with internal parliamentary working procedures.

Gender and formal power

International scholars may be surprised to hear that Sweden has never had a female prime minister. Currently, there are four parties, the Center Party, the Conservative Party, the Green Party and the Feminist Initiative (not in the Riksdag), that have female party leaders. Thus, top positions in Swedish politics are clearly male dominated. This section, however, focuses on gender and formal power in the Riksdag, which is a slightly different matter; not all Swedish party leaders have a seat in the parliament,[1] and it is quite common for cabinet ministers to be recruited from outside of the Riksdag.

A focus on standing committees

All Nordic countries are parliamentary democracies with proportional representation, although they differ, for example, in committee structure. In the Nordic context, committees are most influential in the Swedish parliament (Hagevi 2000, 247). The power of the Riksdag committees stems, among other things, from the fact that committee reports are compulsory on all bills; committees can change bills or make amendments (they also tend to use this right); and they can also initiate bills (ibid., 243). In periods of minority government, common in Sweden, the power of the Riksdag committees become even stronger. Power also stems from the fact that regular committee meetings are closed and that the committee system in Sweden has been stable for some time. Moreover, Swedish MPs clearly perceive the committees to have an impact on decision making in the Riksdag; the committees are ranked as number three out of eight different groups and bodies, just after the cabinet and parliamentary party leaders, when it concerns perceived influence (Esaiasson and Holmberg 1996, 219).

The fact that standing committees are influential motivates a comprehensive analysis of changes over time. In this section, we shall start to look at developments concerning the proportion of standing committees with a woman as a chair or vice-chair. Since changes in these positions can occur fairly rapidly, Figure 4.1 reports the situation at the beginning of each Riksdag year, 1985–2014 (the Riksdag year begins in October of one year and ends in June the following year). Until the 2006 election there were 16 standing committees in the Riksdag, and thereafter 15. The results in Figure 4.1 should be read as the percentage of committees with a woman as chair (solid line) and the percentage of committees with a woman as president, that is, either as chair or vice-chair (dotted line).

Internal parliamentary working procedures 63

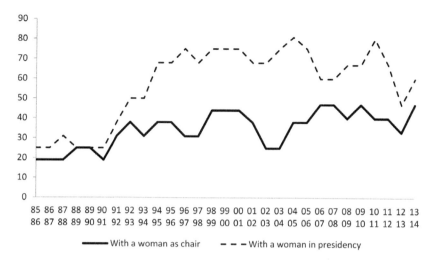

Figure 4.1 Percentage of standing committees in the Swedish parliament with a woman in the presidency, 1985–2014
(Parliamentary membership rolls)

The results in Figure 4.1 display a rather bumpy picture. The proportion of committees with a woman as chair has been at most 47 percentas it was in the Riksdag years 2006/07, 2007/08, 2009/10 and 2013/14. The lowest proportions, 19 percent, are found in the Riksdag years 1985/86 to 1987/88, and 1990/91. To continue, the proportion of committees with a woman in the presidency has at most been 80 percent: Riksdag years 2004/05 and 2010/11. The lowest proportions, 25 percent, are found in the Riksdag years 1985/86, 1986/87, 1988/89, and 1990/91. Analyzed in more detail, the data show that something happened in the 1994 election; since then the proportion of committees with a woman in the presidency has been at least 60 percent (with the exception of the Riksdag year 2012/13). This means that most, but not all, standing committees have experienced a fairly long period with a woman in a leadership position, as either chair or vice-chair.

We shall now turn to an analysis of gender structures linked to areas of responsibility. In Sweden the parliamentary standing committees roughly reflect areas of responsibility attached to cabinet ministers, even though there is no total correspondence. For example, during the 2010/14 term there was a minister for finance in the cabinet and a corresponding committee on finance in the Riksdag. However, there was a minister for health and insurance affairs in the cabinet, but in the Riksdag there were two committees in that area of responsibility, the committee on social affairs and the committee on social insurance. There was also, for example, a minister for gender equality in the cabinet, but in the Riksdag issues of gender equality were handled by the committee on the labor market.

The number of regular committee members is typically 15 or 17 in each committee, and seats are distributed proportionally to parties. In the end, it is the parties themselves that decide who should represent them.[2] The informal norm is that members should only serve as a regular member on one committee at a time (Hagevi 2000, 246).

Table 4.1 shows the proportion of women among regular MPs in Riksdag committees for each term 1971–2014. The committees have been divided into four groups with four committees in each: social welfare, culture/law, basic functions, and economy/technology.[3] For each group, the average proportion of women is compared to the average proportion of women in the entire committee organization. A plus sign means that the proportion of women in that committee group is higher than the average among all committees, while a minus sign denotes that the proportion of women is lower than the average among all committees. An effect measurement is also shown in Table 4.1, which is the most interesting measure to watch. A high figure indicates a major gender effect on committee assignments, whereas a low figure indicates a minor effect.

If we begin with the effect measurement, it shows that the gender effect was greatest in the 1988/91 and 1991/94 terms (effect measurement 19 for both periods) and that it was lowest for the 2006/10 and 2010/14 terms (effect measurement 5). In a review of the comparison measurements, the most prominent result is a pattern of overrepresentation (plus signs) of women on committees in the area of social welfare, and underrepresentation (minus signs) in the economy/technology area. The proportion of women in the culture/law and basic functions areas is comparatively close to the average for the committee organization as a whole.

Figure 4.2 builds on the results in Table 4.1 and focuses on committees in the areas of social welfare and economy/technology. The straight horizontal center line on the chart represents the percentage of women in the committee organization as a whole; a line above the center line shows overrepresentation, and a line below the centerline shows underrepresentation.

What becomes immediately apparent in Figure 4.2 is how particular gender structures emerge in the 1980s and early 1990s and then subside. The 1994 election is a notable breaking point. Also noteworthy is that the lines nearly converge in the 2006/10 term.

A study of gender gaps in preferences for taking part on the committees in the Riksdag (Wängnerud 1998, 89) shows that the changes in actual assignments that took place after the 1994 election did not correspond to any significant changes in preferences: in 1985 42 percent of women MPs preferred on taking part on a committee in the social welfare group and in 1994 the percentage was 39 percent, which is almost the same level (corresponding figures among men MPs were 15 percent in 1985 and 16 percent in 1994). Results from qualitative interviews show that the sharp decline in actual assignments (Figure 4.2) after the 1994 election was mainly a result of conscious acts on behalf of the party leadership (Wängnerud 1998). As discussed in previous chapters, the

Table 4.1 Proportion of women on standing committees, 1971–2014

Term	Social welfare % Women	Social welfare Compare	Culture/law % Women	Culture/law Compare	Basic functions % Women	Basic functions Compare	Economy/technology % Women	Economy/technology Compare	Average all 16	Effect measure
1971/73	20	+5	24	+9	9	-6	5	-10	15	10
1974/76	22	+6	23	+7	15	-1	5	-11	16	10
1976/79	19	0	26	+7	24	+5	8	-11	19	6
1979/82	29	+7	27	+5	21	-1	13	-9	22	9
1982/85	39	+13	34	+8	20	-6	12	-14	26	16
1985/88	42	+13	36	+7	22	-7	18	-11	29	14
1988/91	54	+19	41	+6	24	-11	21	-14	35	19
1991/94	49	+16	41	+8	25	-8	15	-18	33	19
1994/98	47	+3	49	+5	42	-2	36	-8	44	7
1998/02	50	+5	50	+5	40	-5	42	-3	45	6
2002/06	56	+9	44	-3	44	-3	45	-2	47	6
2006/10	51	+4	48	+1	44	-3	43	-4	47	5
2010/14	49	+5	44	0	44	0	40	-4	44	5

(Parliamentary membership rolls)

The policy area of social welfare includes the following committees: social affairs, social insurance, labor market, and education; culture/law includes cultural affairs, justice, law, and constitutional affairs; basic functions includes foreign affairs, defense, environment, agriculture, and housing; economy/technology includes finance, tax, business, and transport. The figures in the table show an average for each term and include regular committee members. The comparison measure compares the proportion of women MPs on committees in each policy area with the average proportion of women in the entire committee organization: (+) denotes that women MPs are overrepresented in relation to the average and (-) that they are underrepresented. The number of regular MPs in each committee is typically 15 in the sessions 1971–73 to 1985–88 and 1991–94, and 17 in the sessions 1988–91 and 1994–98 to 2010–14. In 2006 the committees on law and housing were collapsed into one committee (in the table this new committee is included in both the categories "culture/law" and "basic functions"). The effect measurement shows the average difference that emerges upon a staged comparison of the four committee groups. The calculation is made as follows (example from the term 1971–73): [(20 - 24 = -4) + (20 - 9 = 11) + (20 - 5 = 15) + (24 - 5 = 19)] / 6 = 10.

feminist network the Support Stockings, was active in the 1994 election campaign in Sweden, and the established parties were pushed into implementing visible changes in the area of gender equality. The qualitative interviews underpin the notion that this applied not only to the external party lists but also to internal bodies of power in the Riksdag, such as the standing committees.

Before we move on to gender gaps in informal power we shall take a look at the proportion of women in the category labeled "power position" in the regression analyses in previous chapters (see Table 2.2 and 3.2). This category includes all MPs who are members of parliamentary party executives (party boards), leaders of parliamentary party groups, and/or chairs or vice-chairs of standing committees. This category consists of roughly 30 percent of all MPs, and the data at hand cover the period 1988–2010. The results (not displayed in a table) show that the proportion of women who enter this group is as high as that of men, but as the number of women is lower than the number of men in the Riksdag as a whole, this means that women, even if they are proportionally represented, end up in a minority position.

MPs' assessments of their personal contact

It is a challenge to measure influence and power. Data on formal positions like committee assignments may tell one story, whereas indicators on informal power may tell another. The Swedish Parliamentary Surveys include questions on MPs' personal contact with a number of powerful individuals such as cabinet ministers.

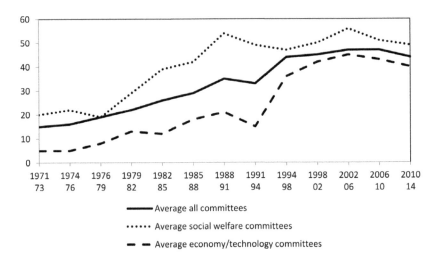

Figure 4.2 Proportion of women in social welfare committees compared with economy/technology committees, 1971–2014
The chart is based on results in Table 4.1.

Table 4.2 reports Swedish MPs' assessments of their personal contact with cabinet ministers, senior government ministry officials, representatives of the party organization in the constituency, and representatives of the party organization outside the constituency. Those included in Table 4.2 report having personal contact at least once a week and can thus be seen as MPs who are part of influential policy networks.

The first thing to note is that comparatively few MPs have regular personal contact with cabinet ministers or senior government ministry officials. The average for cabinet ministers is 17 percent for the period 1985–2010, and the corresponding figure for senior government ministry officials is an average of 13 percent. These figures should be compared with the proportion of MPs reporting regular personal contact with representatives of the party organization in the constituency: on average, 70 percent of MPs report such contact for the period 1985–2010.

Most important to note in Table 4.2, however, is that gender gaps are small and do not in any systematic way go in one direction; some years more women than men MPs report having regular contact, and other years it is the other way round. The only tendency displayed in Table 4.2 is that male MPs seem to have more contact with representatives of the party organization outside the constituency, but except for 1985, gender gaps are fairly small.

Gender and informal power

The research group responsible for the Swedish Parliamentary Surveys has varied over time, and, as discussed in Appendix I on methodology, the composition of this group matters for the type of survey questions included. A main thread in all surveys is questions related to political representation – that is, measures on priorities and attitudes that are comparable to priorities and attitudes among citizens. On some occasions, however, questions related to internal parliamentary working conditions have been included, and in the subsequent sections I shall focus on two such questions: The first question asks members to assess the Riksdag's working conditions, the working conditions within their own party group, their personal working conditions, and (on one survey occasion) the working conditions within the standing committees. The second question used in the forthcoming analyses asks members to assess their ability to make an impact on their own party group's position. The question on impact relates to the members' own areas of expertise.[4]

Assessments of working conditions

Table 4.3 reports Swedish MPs' assessments of working conditions in the Riksdag and in their own party groups, as well as their personal working conditions and the working conditions in standing committees.

I shall start by commenting on the results for 1988: At that time very few MPs, less than one third of all respondents, were satisfied with the working

Table 4.2 Swedish MPs' assessments of their personal contact with cabinet ministers, government officials, and party organizations, 1985–2010 (% reporting contact at least once a week)

Year	Cabinet ministers Wom.	Cabinet ministers Men	Cabinet ministers Diff.	Senior government ministry officials Wom.	Senior government ministry officials Men	Senior government ministry officials Diff.	Party organization in the constituency Wom.	Party organization in the constituency Men	Party organization in the constituency Diff.	Party organization outside the constituency Wom.	Party organization outside the constituency Men	Party organization outside the constituency Diff.
1985	15	15	0	11	12	-1	78	77	+1	9	20	-11
1988	12	13	-1	10	9	+1	63	65	-2	10	6	+4
1994	24	28	-4	17	18	-1	75	78	-3	11	15	-4
1998	16	14	+2	11	9	+2	72	78	-6	9	16	-7
2002	18	18	0	18	14	+4	67	65	+2	8	14	-6
2010	13	15	-2	13	14	-1	62	67	-5	10	12	-2

(Swedish Parliamentary Surveys, Department of Political Science, University of Gothenburg)

conditions in the parliament or with their personal working conditions. In the 1988 survey the party groups stands out as the least problematic arena. However, this pattern is no longer true. Between 1988 and 2006 the proportion satisfied increases dramatically in the categories labeled "parliamentary working conditions" and "personal working conditions," but remains stable in the category "party group working conditions." Between 1988 and 2006 there was a major change in the administrative support to members of the Riksdag, and standard parliamentary procedures, such as the schedule for meetings in committees and the chamber, were revised (Riksdag report 2000/01:RSI).

The most consistent gender gap, with women as the least satisfied group, is found in the assessments of working conditions in the party groups: the gender gap was 10 percentage points in 1988 and 2006, and 11 percentage points in 2010. Women are also a bit more critical than men about their personal working conditions, but when it comes to working conditions in the parliament and the standing committees there is no clear pattern showing women to be the least satisfied group.

We shall now turn to a multivariate regression analysis to capture more carefully variation across time and across different groups of MPs. The dependent variable in Table 4.4 is a dichotomy separating satisfied MPs from the rest (see Table 4.3), and the independent variables included are gender, party affiliation, age, parliamentary experience, education, and whether the MPs hold a distinguished power position. The focus is on MPs' assessments of working conditions in their own party groups. This focus is motivated by the significant role that political parties play in parliamentary processes.

The first thing to note in Table 4.4 is that in 1988 none of the independent variables shows a significant effect. This means that explanations for variation in satisfaction lie outside the model; the factor that is closest to being significant is, however, gender (sig. 0.12). In 2006 and 2010 there is a significant effect of gender, and in 2010 there is also a clear result showing that party affiliation is significant: MPs within the Conservative Party (which is the biggest party in the governing coalition for the 2010/14 term) are the most satisfied. In fact, the group most satisfied is that of male MPs within the Conservative Party.

More detailed analyses have been conducted, and they show no consistent patterns that relate to MPs' age, experience, education, or power position. A path analysis[5] has been conducted to find out to what extent the effect of gender displayed in Table 4.4 is transmitted through the party group. In the path analysis the parties are divided into two groups: the center-right bloc (the Conservative Party, the Liberal Party, the Center Party, and the Christian Democratic Party); and the left-green bloc (the Social Democratic Party, the Left Party, and the Green Party). Previous research shows that members in opposition parties tend to be more critical and also voluntarily leave the parliament to a higher degree than members belonging to parties in government (Ahlbäck Öberg et al. 2007, 51). In 1988 center-right parties were in opposition, whereas they belonged to the governing coalition in 2006 and 2010.[6]

Table 4.3 Swedish MPs' assessments of working conditions, 1988, 2006, and 2010 (% satisfied)

Year	Parliamentary working conditions			Party group working conditions			Personal working conditions			Standing committee working conditions		
	Wom.	Men	Diff.	Wom.	Men	Diff.	Wom.	Men	Diff.	Wom.	Men	Diff.
1988	16	27	-11	46	56	-10	28	32	-4	–	–	–
2006	68	61	+7	52	62	-10	71	84	-13	76	73	+3
2010	70	74	-4	52	63	-11	76	83	-7	–	–	–

(Swedish Parliamentary Surveys, Department of Political Science, University of Gothenburg)

The question reads: "Generally speaking, what do you think of your personal working conditions in parliament, the Riksdag's working conditions, and your own group's working conditions?" The following response alternatives were offered: "Good as it is," "Mostly good as it is," "Needs improvement in several areas," "Needs fundamental change." Included in the table are percentages answering "Good as it is" or "Mostly good as it is" (categories merged).

Table 4.4 Determinants of Swedish MPs' assessments of party group working conditions, 1988, 2006, and 2010 (logistic regression)

	1988 B	SE	Sig.	2006 B	SE	Sig.	2010 B	SE	Sig.
Gender	-0.43	0.28	0.12	-0.40	0.24	0.09	-0.59	0.27	0.03
Lft	–	–	–	-0.10	0.52	0.83	-1.85	0.58	0.00
SocDem	-0.22	0.36	0.54	-0.36	0.33	0.27	-2.16	0.39	0.00
Grn	–	–	–	-1.25	0.59	0.03	-0.70	0.55	0.19
Cen	-0.37	0.47	0.43	0.04	0.47	0.92	-2.02	0.59	0.00
Lib	-0.08	0.45	0.98	-1.03	0.51	0.04	-1.03	0.57	0.07
ChrDem	n.a.	n.a.	n.a.	-0.11	0.50	0.81	-1.24	0.58	0.03
SweDem	n.a.	n.a.	n.a.	n.a.	n.a.	n.a.	-1.45	0.75	0.05
Con (reference)									
Age	0.00	0.02	0.69	0.00	0.01	0.98	0.00	0.01	0.54
Experience	0.00	0.02	0.88	0.00	0.02	0.94	0.01	0.02	0.55
Education	-0.33	0.28	0.24	-0.73	0.30	0.01	-0.18	0.32	0.57
Power position	0.25	0.30	0.41	0.08	0.30	0.79	0.03	0.31	0.91
Constant	0.93	1.05	0.37	1.33	0.68	0.05	1.49	0.76	0.05
Nagelkerke	0.11			0.08			0.21		

(Swedish Parliamentary Surveys, Department of Political Science, University of Gothenburg)

See Table 4.3 for information on the question asked. See Appendices for information on the categories. A – means that all answers are in one category.

The results of the path analysis show that in 2010 the effect of gender is to a large extent transmitted through the party groups: Women are more numerous in left-green parties than in center-right parties, and women in left-green parties are also the most critical.[7] The results for 2010 can be illustrated by a table chart displaying gender on one dimension and bloc affiliation on the other (Table 4.4.1). The following table includes the percentage satisfied for four groups: men MPs in the left-green bloc, men MPs in the center-right bloc, women MPs in the left-green bloc, and women MPs in the center-right bloc.

The results in Table 4.4.1 show that male MPs in the left-green bloc are less satisfied than male MPs in the center-right bloc; the difference is 24 percentage points, but the gap between female MPs in the two blocs is much wider: 40 percentage points. Given the fact that the number of women is exceptionally high in left-green parties (see Table 2.1), and given the strong commitment to gender equality in these parties (see Chapter 2 of this book), this result is surprising. Before I comment further on these results, let us look at the indicator on informal power that deals with MPs' perceived ability to make an impact on their own party groups.

Assessment of the ability to make an impact on the MPs' own party groups' positions

One could easily imagine that there should be a clear correlation between MPs' ability to make an impact on their own party groups' positions and satisfaction with working conditions in the party groups, but the following analyses illustrate that there is no simple correlation between those two phenomena. Table 4.5 shows Swedish MPs' assessments of their ability to impact their own party groups' positions.

First of all, the results show that the vast majority of MPs – women as well as men – perceive their ability to make an impact as either "very" or "fairly" good. On all survey occasions less than 6 percent answer "not so good." Second, it is only in 1988 and 2006 that the results show an expected gender gap, with fewer women than men answering "very good." In 1988 the gender gap is 10 percentage points, and in 2010, 8 percentage points. In 2006 the gender gap is smaller, 2 percentage points, and the results show that more women than men perceive their ability to make an impact as very good.

Table 4.4.1 Proportion satisfied with their own party group working conditions in 2010

	Men MPs	Women MPs	Diff.
Left-green bloc	50%	33%	+17
Center-right bloc	74%	73%	+1
Diff.	−24	−40	

Table 4.5 Swedish MPs' assessments of their ability to impact their own party groups' positions (%)

	Very good			Fairly good			Not so good		
Year	Wom.	Men	Diff.	Wom.	Men	Diff.	Wom.	Men	Diff.
1988	44	54	-10	54	44	+10	2	2	0
2006	54	52	+2	44	43	+1	2	5	-3
2010	49	57	-8	47	40	+7	4	3	+1

(Swedish Parliamentary Surveys, Department of Political Science, University of Gothenburg)

The question reads: "How do you rate your ability to impact your party group's positions on various issues?" The table reports assessments on "Issues within my own area of expertise." The following response alternatives were offered: "Very good," "Fairly good," "Fairly bad," "Very bad." The category "Not so good" includes response alternatives "fairly bad" and "very bad" (categories merged).

The next step is, as in the previous section, to look at results from a multivariate regression analysis. The dependent variable in Table 4.6 is a dichotomy between respondents answering "very good" and the rest (see Table 4.5). The independent variables included, besides gender and party affiliation, are age, parliamentary experience, education, and whether the MPs hold a distinguished power position.

I would like to start by drawing attention to the fact that the category "power position" shows a clear and consistent effect: this means that MPs who are assigned to a distinguished power position do perceive, to a large extent, their ability to impact their own party groups' positions as "very good." The results in Table 4.6 show that gender has a significant negative effect in 1988 and 2010; however, additional analyses show that the single largest effect on perceived possibilities for making an impact stems from wheter or not one is in a power position.

In accordance with the analysis on satisfaction with working conditions in the party groups, consider Table 4.6.1, displaying gender in one dimension and bloc affiliation in the other. The results show percentages answering "very good" on the question about their ability to make an impact, in four groups: men MPs in the left-green bloc, men MPs in the center-right bloc, women MPs in the left-green bloc, and women MPs in the center-right bloc.

The highest proportion answering "very good," 61 percent, is found among male MPs who belong to the center-right bloc (it could be added that male MPs in the Conservative Party constitute the group with the most positive view on their ability to have an impact). However, a comparatively high proportion, 52 percent, is also found among female MPs in the left-green bloc. In 2010 the proportion answering "very good" is on the same level, 46 percent, among male MPs in the left-green bloc and female MPs in the center right-bloc.

Table 4.6 Determinants of Swedish MPs' assessments of their ability to impact their own party groups' positions, 1988, 2006, and 2010 (logistic regression)

	1988			2006			2010		
	B	SE	Sig.	B	SE	Sig.	B	SE	Sig.
Gender	-0.60	0.32	0.06	0.06	0.26	0.81	-0.45	0.27	0.10
Lft	1.54	1.14	0.17	0.87	0.57	0.12	0.72	0.59	0.22
SocDem	-1.02	0.41	0.01	0.30	0.35	0.38	-0.33	0.36	0.35
Grn	–	–	–	1.32	0.62	0.03	0.66	0.55	0.23
Cen	0.89	0.54	0.10	1.94	0.56	0.00	1.08	0.67	0.10
Lib	0.50	0.50	0.31	0.79	0.55	0.15	0.38	0.61	0.52
ChrDem	n.a.	n.a.	n.a.	1.33	0.53	0.01	0.59	0.60	0.31
SweDem	n.a.	n.a.	n.a.	n.a.	n.a.	n.a.	1.04	0.82	0.20
Con (reference)									
Age	-0.06	0.02	0.00	-0.06	0.01	0.00	-0.02	0.01	0.12
Experience	0.09	0.03	0.00	0.09	0.03	0.00	0.08	0.03	0.00
Education	-0.14	0.32	0.65	-0.15	0.30	0.60	0.53	0.33	0.11
Power position	1.44	0.35	0.00	1.23	0.33	0.00	1.50	0.34	0.00
Constant	2.50	1.21	0.03	1.74	0.73	0.01	-0.07	0.75	0.92
Nagelkerke	0.34			0.26			0.28		

(Swedish Parliamentary Surveys, Department of Political Science, University of Gothenburg)

See Table 4.5 for information on the question asked. See Appendices for information on the categories. A – means that all answers are in one category.

Table 4.6.1 Proportion answering "very good" to the question about MPs' ability to impact their own party groups in 2010

	Men MPs	Women MPs	Diff.
Left-green bloc	46%	52%	-6
Center-right bloc	61%	46%	+15
Diff.	-15	+6	

What's wrong with parliamentary party groups?

I shall not try to push the data from the Swedish Parliamentary Surveys too far. What the results from previous sections show is that there is no clear correlation between the MPs' ability to impact their own party groups' positions and satisfaction with working conditions in the party groups. In order to shed further light on the puzzle as to why women are less satisfied than men with working conditions in the party groups, I shall turn to data from the project on turnover in the Riksdag, mentioned in the introduction to this chapter.

As already stated, it was the speaker of the Riksdag who initiated the project on turnover, but the research group was provided a free hand when it came to design, data collection and publication of results.[8] The data collected consist of a survey of all individuals who were members of parliament during the 1994/98 term, but who were no longer members after the 1998 election, totaling 129 persons. In addition, semi-structured qualitative interviews were conducted with a smaller group of individuals, in total 37 persons. Of the 129 persons who left the Riksdag in the 1988 election, 44 were excluded due to election results. The rest had, in advance of the election, signaled that they wanted to resign.[9]

The main result of the project on turnover was the finding of a generational gap: older MPs tend to leave the Riksdag after a long career, and to them, their time in parliament is "a jewel in the crown." Younger MPs tend to be more critical of their time in parliament, but most remarkable was that younger MPs, after a comparatively short period, felt that they "had done their job." The analyses show that to young MPs their time in parliament was not a jewel in the crown but one of many options to make an impact. Younger MPs seemed to be constantly reevaluating their mission and looking for the optimal arena to fulfill their goals: this arena could be the parliament, a local council, an international organization, or an interest group. The analyses show that younger MPs who left the Riksdag did not necessarily leave politics (Ahlbäck Öberg et al. 2007).

Besides the discovery of a generational gap, the main finding of the project on turnover was that women MPs were more critical than men MPs of their time in parliament. In accordance with previous results, it was found that women in opposition parties were the most critical. In the project on turnover there are few signs of women being less capable in their role as MPs. In contrast, the results show that more men than women express feelings of inadequacy when they explain their decision not to stand for another term (Ahlbäck Öberg et al. 2007, 173).

We now turn to the qualitative interviews to find a deeper understanding of dissatisfaction with the party groups – in particular, two rather extensive examples of reasoning among young female MPs who voluntarily left the Riksdag. The first comes from an interview with a woman from the Conservative Party. In the following quote the interviewer (Q) is focusing on the respondent's (R) perception of the possibility of combining the role as an MP with other aspects of life:[10]

Q: What one starts to think of is whether there is something in the parliamentary structure that encourages or prevents certain ways of being [as an MP]. Did you find the parliament's way of functioning encouraged you to only engage in parliamentary work?

R: Yeah. I almost feel that. Not the least ... maybe not the parliamentary structure, but more the party structure – it is often parties that put pressure on external activities. Then there is a fact that there is a difference between being from Stockholm [the capital] and being a traveling member, which I was. For those who are traveling, it is always very pressing to be in Stockholm mid-week, and then when you come home to the constituency you should take back what has been removed from them ... In fact, I spent more and more time in Stockholm at the end. Then when I knew I would be leaving [the Riksdag] and all that stuff, then it got easier, to have life in one place.

Q: Is there anything you think that the parties could do better, to help one to combine different things?

R: Yes, I think so. One can find good basic structures that take into account that we need to be people too, not to go on [as politicians] for what seems like forever.

Q: Is there something that comes to your mind that you feel you could have done differently, when you came into parliament?

R: Well, not like that one should change anything in the organization, but it is more like ... I think it is more of an attitude from older colleagues, and from the constituency side; they need to understand that the main rule cannot be that the party is entitled to all evenings and even weekends. The principle must be to try to create some balance in life, and therefore it is okay to say no. I cannot see that it would be ... the structure – it is more about the attitude.

What is highlighted in the quote, and this is a recurrent theme in the interviews, is that parliamentary work is just one dimension of the role as an elected representative; other dimensions have to do with the work in the constituency and also outreach activities such as appearing in the media. The node for most of these different activities is the party and not the parliament, as such. Another recurrent theme in the qualitative interviews has to do with underlying norms, that older colleagues expect younger ones to be loyal party workers just as they are. The next example comes from an interview with a woman from the Center Party which also highlights the importance of attitudes of older colleagues. The following response comes to a question in the interviews that has to do with problems of recruiting new members to political parties:

Q: We can conclude that the parties today have problems recruiting members. And then, I wonder if you have any idea of how to attract others to become politically active?

R: Yes. I think one must, I think, first, you must accept that people might not want to be in [politics] for 10 years or 20 years, but they may put it this way, "I have four years of my life where I want to get involved in politics," and then you [the parties] should take advantage of them now and not let people wait, but give them duties, let them be part. I think that is important, so you don't need to wait until you get tired ... I cannot consider it as dropping out; if you actually spent four years of your spare time, then you have made an effort. And then it may be so that you [the political party] would like that they [MPs] are around for a while, because that's when they start getting better ... but I think it's important that you can do things for a limited time and feel that it's okay, and that you have done it, just like with any job. So, a little more of the attitude that one hasn't failed, if after four or five years one says that now I need to step down, for now I want to do something else.

Q: Do you think the Riksdag can do something to make it more attractive to be politically active?

R: Actually, I think maybe it's not the parliament's task ... actually there are the political parties and society in general as well, because it's not only the political parties' task.

The respondent above widens the perspective and includes attitudes in society in general. The important point, however, is that both of these respondents, in a similar way, point to certain norms that characterize the inner life of parliamentary party groups. Norms that have to do with expectations of what a "good" MP is. The interpretation I make is that they perceive a good MP to be one who is loyal to the party, maybe not so much in terms of attitudes and opinions, but in terms of standing up for their party in all kinds of settings and in a long-term perspective.

In our study on turnover we do not find support for the assumption that more women than men choose to leave the parliament for family reasons. In a factor analysis a factor labeled "tired of party politics" turns out to be strongest among women. It refers to answers to an open-ended question in the survey that brought up aspects such as panjandrum, decision making behind closed doors, and party whips (Ahlbäck Öberg et al. 2007, 170).[11] One example from the open-ended question in the survey is:

[There was] strong internal strife – deceit and dishonesty within the party. To some extent disappointment over how undemocratic "my own party" was behind closed doors. A few men at the top were allowed to control too much. No teamwork in the parliamentary group. Everyone struggles for themselves; they had resigned – discouraged, no belief in the future.[12]

I believe that the data from the study on turnover, taken together, contribute to an increased focus on norms of appropriate behavior that are not directly linked to gender. These norms do not ascribe a typical feminine role to women, such as being caring or taking responsibility for policy areas dealing with children or the family. The norms displayed are linked to a certain political role, that of a loyal party worker. In our study more women than men oppose this norm, and in this way it can be said to be indirectly linked to gender.

Gender-specific obstacles?

"Masculinity" and "femininity" can take many forms. The point made in feminist institutionalism is that the roles women and men are able to play within legislatures are, at least partially, predetermined. Bolzendahl (2014) finds, in her study on legislative committees in Germany, Sweden, and the United States, a combination of stereotyping and organizational redesign that works to protect masculine privilege. Bolzendahl's way of categorizing the committees is slightly different from mine, but she also finds a pattern of convergence in the Riksdag. This pattern of convergence is one reason for her to classify the Swedish parliament as an egalitarian-trending gendered organization.

I would like to point out that women in the Riksdag reach powerful positions, and the distribution of seats in standing committees has been fairly gender neutral for quite some time. However, women in the Riksdag are still less satisfied than men with the working conditions in the parliamentary party groups. I would like to put a question mark behind the assumption that convergence in terms of areas of responsibility is a core driving force behind a gender-sensitive parliament. My conclusion is that much more focus should be directed toward underlying norms about the "good" politician. The picture that emerges from the analysis in this chapter – of the loyal party worker – may be masculine, but this aspect has received less attention in research than other forms of masculinity.

In the recent Riksdag, in the 2010/14 term, male MPs expressed a wish to sit in committees dealing with social welfare. Results from the Swedish Parliamentary Survey show that 32 percent of male MPs in 2010 preferred a seat in a committee in the category "social welfare." At the same time 29 percent of male MPs preferred a seat in the category "economy/technology." This is a major change; committees dealing with economy/technology used to be totally dominant among male MPs (Wängnerud 1998, 89). Among women, the results for 2010 are equivalent to those from earlier periods: in the 2010 survey 44 percent of female MPs preferred a seat in a committee in the category "social welfare," and 25 percent preferred a seat on the category "economy/technology." These are almost the same levels as in previous years (ibid.).

I believe that we need more information before we can reach a final conclusion on how to evaluate "functional" divisions between women and men in areas such as the standing committees. It may be that we need to do contextual interpretations: under certain circumstances it may be wise for women to concentrate on social welfare committees.

My main conclusion of the analyses in this chapter is that women in the Riksdag meet certain gender-specific obstacles and these obstacles are linked to norms of appropriate behavior in the party groups, which, in one way, makes them particularly important to highlight, since the party groups are decisive for the everyday lives of elected representatives. At the same time it should be noted that women in the Riksdag do not assess their prospects of making an impact to be any different from how their male colleagues assess theirs. Most MPs perceive the possibility of their making an impact as either very or fairly good when it comes to their own areas of expertise. Thus, the obstacles are not so severe that they prevent women from having power and influence.

Notes

1 It happens that party leaders do not have a seat in the parliament; however, this is not common. A prominent example is Stefan Löfven, who in 2012 was recruited as leader for the Social Democratic Party. Löfven came from a position in the labor movement, and the practical consequence for the Social Democratic Party has been that between 2012 and 2014 their party leader has not been able to take part in the debates in the Riksdag. Instead, the group leader in the Riksdag, Mikael Damberg, participated in the most important debates.
2 In most parties members are able to express a wish for a certain committee assignment. About half of the MPs get a seat on their first choice of committee. In 1985 and 1988 fewer women than men got a seat on their first choice of committee. However, the Swedish Parliamentary Surveys show that this changed in 1994, at which time 49 percent among women MPs and 48 percent among men MPs got a seat on their first choice of committee (Wängnerud 1998, 99).
3 This categorization builds on a continuum along the dimension reproduction–production (Wängnerud 1998, 209).
4 Very few MPs report having impact outside their own area of expertise.
5 This is not perfectly correct from a methodological point of view, since the dependent variable is dichotomous rather than being a continuum.
6 The Left Party and the Green Party, before the 2014 election, had never been part of the Swedish cabinet. However, they are usually seen as "support parties" for the Social Democratic Party. After the 2014 election a minority government was formed by the Social Democratic Party and the Green Party.
7 This result is, however, not equally clear in 1988 or 2006.

8 The project was a collaboration between Shirin Ahlbäck Öberg, Jörgen Hermansson and myself, at the Department of Political Science, University of Uppsala, Sweden.
9 The focus of this study was to a large extent on internal parliamentary working conditions. The survey was sent out in December 1998, about three months after the election. The response rate was 88.4 percent. The semi-structured interviews took place in 2000 and the design was based on four categories: young vs. old MPs, and MPs who had left vs. those still in the Riksdag. For each category "matching" was done, taking into account gender and party affiliation.
10 I personally translated the interviews. Minor editing has been done to facilitate understanding. Transcriptions of the interviews (in Swedish) are kept in my archives.
11 The other factors included in the analysis were "been in parliament long enough," "left because of private life," "have done my community service," and "insufficient time and resources."
12 The question posed reads, "In your own words, what was the reason not to run for a seat in parliament in the election of September 20, 1998?"

Bibliography

Ahlbäck Öberg, Shirin, Jörgen Hermansson and Lena Wängnerud. 2007. *Exit riksdagen*. Malmö: Liber.

Bækgaard, Martin and Ukrik Kjær. 2012. "The Gendered Division of Labor in Assignments to Political Committees: Discrimination or Self-Selection in Danish Local Politics?" *Politics & Gender* 8: 465–482.

Bolzendahl, Catherine. 2014. "Opportunities and Expectations: The Gendered Organization of Legislative Committees in Germany, Sweden, and the United States." *Gender & Society*, published online August 1, 2014.

Dahlerup, Drude and Monique Leyenaar, eds. 2013. *Breaking Male Dominance in Old Democracies*. Oxford: Oxford University Press.

Esaiasson, Peter and Sören Holmberg. 1996. *Representation from Above. Members of Parliament and Representative Democracy in Sweden*. Aldershot: Dartmouth.

Haavio-Mannila, Elina et al. 1983. *Det uferdige demokartiet. Kvinner i nordisk politikk*. Oslo: Nordisk ministerråd. (Published in English as *Unfinished Democracy: Women in Nordic Politics*. Oxford: Pergamon Press, 1985.)

Hagevi, Magnus. 2000. "Nordic Light on Committee Assignments." In *Beyond Westminster and Congress: The Nordic Experience*, ed. Peter Esaiasson and Knut Heidar. Columbus: Ohio State University Press.

Heath, Roseanna M., Leslie A. Schwindt-Bayer and Michelle Taylor-Robinson. 2005. "Women on the Sidelines: Women's Representation on Committees in Latin American Legislatures." *American Journal of Political Science* 49(2): 420–436.

Kathlene, Lyn. 1994. "Power and Influence in State Legislative Policymaking: The Interaction of Gender and Position in Committee Hearing Debates." *American Political Science Review* 88(3): 560–576.

Krook, Mona Lena and Fiona Mackay, eds. 2010. *Gender, Politics and Institutions: Towards a Feminist Intuitionalism*. Basingstoke and New York: Palgrave Macmillan.

Lovenduski, Joni. 2005. *Feminizing Politics*. Cambridge: Polity Press.

Reingold, Beth. 2000. *Representing Women: Sex, Gender, and Legislative Behavior in Arizona and California*. Chapel Hill: University of North Carolina Press.

Skjeie, Hege. 1992. *Den politiske betydningen av kjønn. En studie av norsk topp-politikk.* Rapport 92:11. PhD diss.. Oslo: Inst. Samfunnsforskning.

Thomas, Susan. 1994. *How Women Legislate.* Oxford: Oxford University Press.

Wängnerud, Lena. 1998. *Politikens andra sida. Om kvinnorepresentation i Sveriges Riksdag.* PhD diss., University of Göteborg.

5 Room for women's interests and concerns

"Welfare works," conclude Frances Rosenbluth, Rob Salmond, and Michael Thies in an article from 2006. The aim of the study was to find an explanation for Scandinavian exceptionalism – why the number of women elected to parliaments in this part of the world is so high. The core variable is a measure of nonmilitary government expenditure (as a percentage of gross domestic product – GDP). Using worldwide data, Rosenbluth and colleagues are able to show a strong correlation with the proportion of lower house members who are women. Sweden tops lists of both the highest number of women elected and the highest nonmilitary government expenditure (Rosenbluth *et al.* 2006, 173).

Perhaps most interesting in the study, though, is the suggestion of the core mechanism at work: Rosenbluth and colleagues argue that the key link resides in welfare state policies that: (i) free women to enter the paid workforce; (ii) provide public sector jobs that disproportionately employ women; and (iii) change the political interests of working women enough to create an ideological gender gap. The assumption is that these features create incentives for political parties to compete for the female vote, and one way that they do so is by including more and more women in their party delegations (Rosenbluth et al. 2006, 165).

Data on party choice in Sweden support the assumption of an ideological gender gap. Since the 1979 election significantly fewer women than men have voted for the Conservative Party; the biggest gender gap so far was noted in the 2010 election, when 35 percent of men but only 27 percent of women voted for the Conservative Party (a gap of 8 percentage points). However, the Conservative Party also includes more and more women in their party delegation; after the 2014 election the presence of women in the Conservative Party group was 52 percent (Table 2.1). Thus, there is something missing in the story linking ideological gender gaps to the recruitment of women into party delegations. To bring women forward in party delegations is no "quick fix" for attracting female votes.

The focus of this chapter is on *the amount of room available for women's interests and concerns* on the political agenda. The first part of the chapter includes an attempt to capture scope and prominence on an institutional, collective level. We shall see, however, that this is easier said than done, and analyses will rely heavily on data generated through the Swedish Parliamentary Surveys. The questionnaire-based data cover information on priorities, attitudes, and policy promotion. The advantage of the questionnaire-based data is that we can conduct rather sophisticated analyses to investigate *who* is pushing for change consistent with women's interests. A core question is whether we find major differences between or within political parties.

Problems connected with measuring change

The theory of the politics of presence is clearly about change. In a key passage Anne Phillips (1995, 47) argues that gender equality among those elected to office is desirable because of the changes it can bring about: "It is representation ... with a purpose, it aims to subvert or add or transform." The core mechanism at work in the theory of the politics of presence can be likened to an invisible hand; female politicians are expected to be better equipped to represent the interests of female voters because they, at least to some extent, share the same experiences. There are plenty of counter-hypotheses to this expectation – for example, that ideology is what matters in politics, and that parliamentary institutions influence politicians more than politicians are able to influence them (Bolzendahl 2014; Krook and Mackay 2010; Hawkesworth 2005). Some scholars seek to identify a threshold number or a "tipping point" at which the impact of women's presence in parliament becomes apparent. Sandra Grey (2006) has argued that attaining a proportion of 15 percent may allow female politicians to change the political agenda, but 40 percent may be needed for women-friendly policies to be introduced.

The distinction between the political agenda and women-friendly policies is interesting, since it highlights some of the problems connected with measuring change; for example, what should the dependent variable be?[1] If we return to the study by Rosenbluth and colleagues (2006), we find that they use a measure on nonmilitary government expenditure as a core variable. A similar measure is social expenditure as a percentage of GDP. The Organisation for Economic Co-operation and Development (OECD) provides data that make it possible to track changes over time: In 1980 the figure for Sweden was 27.1 percent, whereas the average for all OECD countries was 15.5 percent. In 1995 there was a "peak" in the data on Sweden with 32.0 percent, but in 2013 the figure for Sweden was down to 28.6 percent. In 2013 the average for all OECD countries was 21.9 percent, and four countries precede Sweden in the list for social expenditure: Belgium, Denmark, Finland, and France.[2]

The OECD data show that Sweden, over time, has become less exceptional. In 1980 the gap between social expenditure in Sweden and the OECD average was 11.6 percentage points. In 2013 the corresponding figure was 6.7

percentage points. Moreover, in the 1980s care and services in Sweden were almost exclusively delivered by the public sector. Stefan Svallfors, a prominent scholar of the Swedish welfare state, concludes that the situation now is considerably different, with a substantial proportion of schools, day care centers, and elderly care centers run by private enterprises rather than public organizations (Svallfors 2011, 808). Those services are still funded by taxes and mandatory contributions, but the traditional social democratic welfare state has undergone substantial changes, such as the increased use of market-emulating mechanisms, but also cutbacks in, for example, replacement levels in social insurance (see Svallfors 2011 and references therein).

It is time to remind ourselves of the definition of "women's interests" made earlier in this book. In Chapter 3 it was suggested that the concept of women's interests can be narrowed down to three concerns: the recognition of women as a social category, the acknowledgment of the unequal balance of power between the sexes, and the occurrence of policies designed to increase the self-determination of female citizens. In the context of a Scandinavian welfare state the aspect of self-determination includes policies related to personal integrity and to the conflict between work and family.

The marketization of the welfare state and the cutbacks described by Svallfors (2011) do not, at least in theory, need to be in conflict with women's interests. The core element stipulated in the definition of women's interests is about having significant and meaningful choices. I have argued that in gender-equal democracies, women and men are equally able to choose between political alternatives that address their specific concerns. Thus, the most important dependent variables in this chapter should consist of indicators on choice and politicization.

There is no clear-cut demarcation between the different dimensions included in the definition of women's interests. The first dimension, the recognition of women as a social category, was discussed in Chapter 3 but will be further discussed at the end of this chapter. The second and third dimensions, the acknowledgment of the unequal balance of power between the sexes and the occurrence of policies designed to increase the self-determination of female citizens, are the themes of the next sections.

The acknowledgment of the unequal balance of power between the sexes

The idea behind the second dimension in the definition of women's interests is to find out to what extent elected representatives are willing to push for change. Phillips (2007, 127) assumes that societies will not achieve equality between women and men by simply disregarding gender-related differences. To recognize women as a social category may be a first step toward change, but it is reasonable to believe that to set developments in motion a necessary second step is to acknowledge women as a disadvantaged group.

In Chapter 2 we could see that in the Swedish context a straightforward question on MPs' attitudes toward gender equality does not work very well. In 1994 the Swedish Parliamentary Survey imagined a number of possible future societies. MPs were asked to evaluate the suggestion "to work toward a society with more equality between women and men." The results showed little variation between groups of MPs, and strikingly positive attitudes: Almost all MPs answered that it is a "very good" proposal to strive for more equality (Oskarson and Wängnerud 1996). It is, however, hardly the case that all Swedish MPs are equally keen to push for strengthening the position of women.

The following survey question concerns Swedish MPs' assessment of their personal contact with non-parliamentary women's organizations. The question deals with MPs' contact as politicians and, disregarding how the contact was initiated, how often they have been in touch with a women's organization. Table 5.1 reports answers among women and men in the Riksdag 1985–2010. This indicator captures MPs' willingness to be in touch with organized interests that focus on the situation of women.

The results in Table 5.1 show – and this is quite expected – that more women MPs than men MPs are in regular contact with women's organizations. Almost no men MPs are in contact with women's organizations on a weekly basis; instead, the vast majority of men MPs report having contact "now and then." Roughly 10 percent of women MPs report having contact on a weekly basis, but the proportion is comparatively small at 7 percent in 2010. A downward trend becomes apparent if the categories "at least once a week" and "once or twice per month" are merged: in 1985 at 55 percent of women MPs reported contact on, at minimum, a monthly basis; in 2010 the corresponding figure is 22 percent. The downward trend among women is not "compensated" for by an upward trend among men – quite the opposite. In 2010 the group reporting no contact at all is comparatively large both among men, 30 percent, and among women, 12 percent.

A similar result, pointing to a small group of very engaged female MPs, arises if one looks at an open-ended question in the Swedish Parliamentary Surveys, asking in which area or areas of politics MPs are most interested. MPs could choose any area or areas. Figure 5.1 shows the percentage who answered "gender equality," "women's issues," "quotas," "gender discrimination," or similar answers, merged into one category. The different graphs illustrate answers for all MPs, plus answers for women MPs and men MPs separately.

The results displayed in Figure 5.1 are a bit puzzling: among women there is an upward trend between 1985 and 2002, and then stabilization occurs around the proportion of 14–15 percent. Among men the proportion who have gender equality as an area of personal interest is never impressive: in 1985 and 2002 the proportion is 3 percent, and on the other survey occasions the corresponding figures are 1 percent in 1988, 1994, and 2006, and 0 percent in 2010. In the Riksdag as a whole this means a peak in 2002 but then a

Table 5.1 Swedish MPs' assessment of their personal contact with women's organizations, 1985–2010 (%)

Year	At least once a week Wom.	At least once a week Men	At least once a week Diff.	Once or twice per month Wom.	Once or twice per month Men	Once or twice per month Diff.	Now and then Wom.	Now and then Men	Now and then Diff.	Never Wom.	Never Men	Never Diff.
1985	11	1	+10	44	8	+36	41	77	-36	4	14	-10
1994	12	0	+12	38	4	+34	46	78	-32	4	18	-14
1998	10	1	+9	33	9	+24	52	70	-18	5	20	-15
2002	13	0	+13	28	6	+22	56	80	-24	3	14	-11
2010	7	0	+7	15	5	+10	66	65	+1	12	30	-18

(Swedish Parliamentary Surveys, Department of Political Science, University of Gothenburg)

The question reads: "This question deals with your contact as a politician with various organizations, groups, and authorities in the past year. Disregarding how the contact was initiated, how often have you, in the past year, personally or by letter, been in touch with the organizations, groups or authorities below," (the total number of organizations and so forth listed varies between survey occasions). The following response alternatives were offered: "At least once a week," "Once or twice a month," "A few times," "Occasionally," and "Never." The category "Now and then" includes "A few times" and "Occasionally" (categories merged).

Room for women's interests and concerns 87

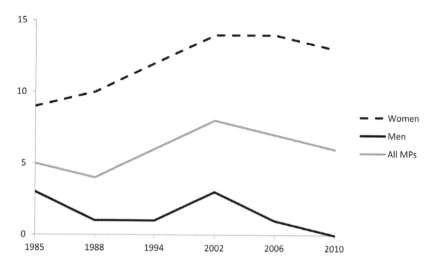

Figure 5.1 Proportion of Swedish MPs who have gender equality as an area of personal interest, 1985–2010 (%)
The question reads: "Which area or areas of politics are you most interested in?" The question was open-ended, and respondents could choose any area or areas. The graph shows the percentages of women and men who answered equality, women's issues, quotas, gender discrimination, or similar answers.
(Swedish Parliamentary Surveys, Department of Political Science, University of Gothenburg)

slight downward trend: in 2010 6 percent of all MPs answered, on the open-ended question, that they have gender equality as an area of personal interest.

In sum, one has to be very careful about which indicators to use when trying to capture the acknowledgment of the unequal balance of power between the sexes. One type of indicator, measuring attitudes toward a possible future society, shows that almost all MPs embrace the idea of more equality between women and men, but another type of indicator, more closely linked to behavior, shows a small group of very engaged MPs, most of whom are women. For the advancement of this book it is most important to note that the results in this section show that there is no indication of a linear process toward increased room for women's interests and concerns.

Policies designed to increase self-determination of female citizens

In Chapter 1 I brought up the debate on self-authorization in the field of women, gender, and politics. In short, I argued that there is a burgeoning strand of research where self-authorization is upgraded, and authorization through general elections devalued, as key components in democratic processes. Dorothy McBride and Amy Mazur (2010, 3) were cited, saying that bringing women's movements into the state is "necessarily about representation" and "making democracies more democratic." I concluded that these authors make the women's movement, not women citizens, into the most important reference point in studies on representation.

The strand of research mentioned above is linked to the ideas brought forward by Michael Saward (2010) in *The Representative Claim*. Karen Celis, Sarah Childs, Johanna Kantola, and Mona Lena Krook (2014) base their analyses on Saward's book in their study of women's interests and how they are constituted in Belgium, Finland, and the United Kingdom. Celis and colleagues state that representative claims may be made by elected and nonelected actors, including state agencies, social movements, international organizations, and celebrities. In addition, Celis et al. (2014, 157) state that these actors do not promote "preexisting interests" but instead draw on their "creative capacity" to offer portrayals of groups and interests. This research group relies on an inductive method, and the content of women's interests is abstracted from the selected material.

The time frame used in the study by Celis and colleagues is 2003–08, and the material consists of various programs where claims are made. A main finding is that there is a rather strong consensus among different actors in each country on what constitutes women's interests: in Belgium all actors included in the analyses mention the gender pay gap, access to the labor market, work-family balance, and participation in decision making; in Finland all actors mention violence against women, trafficking in women and prostitution, gender pay gap/equal pay, women's employment, maternity/paternity/parental leave, and work-family balance; and finally, in the United Kingdom all actors mention violence against women, pensions, gender pay gap, and political representation (Celis *et al.* 2014, 165).

I am not going to exaggerate the difference between the study by Celis and colleagues and my own approach. The use of an inductive method corresponds to what is sometimes presented as "subjectively defined interests" in the field of women, gender, and politics (cf. Wängnerud 2009). In 1992 Hege Skjeie presented an analysis of the "rhetoric on difference" in the Norwegian parliament. Skjeie (1992, 108) asked Norwegian MPs to report what they considered to be "women's interests" and "men's interests." Skjeie found that environmental protection, social and welfare policies, equality, disarmament, and education/culture were considered women's interests, whereas economic and industrial policies, energy, transportation, and national security/foreign affairs were considered men's interests.

My own take on this debate is that we need to be able to differentiate between claims and acts. I see a fundamental difference between studying what actors claim they do, or their rhetoric, and studying the substantive representation of women. For example, the core issue in research on substantive representation does not concern "what women do in parliament," but to what extent women's interests and concerns are present in the political arena. A theoretical a priori definition of women's interests enables a null result – that is, the finding that various actors are self-defined champions of women's interests, but beyond statements in programs they do not act to strengthen the position of women.

I certainly believe that it needs to be recognized that in Western democracies, general elections are an outstanding control station in democratic processes. As stated elsewhere in this book, this way of thinking builds on Hanna Pitkin's (1967, 209) classical definition of political representation: "Representation here means acting in the interest of the represented, in a manner responsive to them." The ballot makes it possible to check levels of support among broad layers of the population. However, what Pitkin suggests is no immediate correspondence between citizens' wishes and the acts of elected representatives. This is about elected representatives not being persistently at odds with the electorate.

The rationale behind using data generated through survey questions

In studies on the United States it is quite common to register legislative voting behavior. Alana Jeydal and Andrew J. Taylor (2003) show that when factors such as seniority and institutional position are taken into account, there is no real, demonstrable difference between the effectiveness of women and men in the US House of Representatives. Two measures of effectiveness are used in their study: the percentage of bills sponsored by a member of Congress that were passed into law, and the distribution among congressional districts of federal money to implement domestic policy. In a similar vein Arturo Vega and Juanita M. Firestone (1995) have examined legislative voting behavior from 1981 to 1992 in the US Congress, and they conclude that "congressional women display distinctive legislative behavior that portends a greater representation of women and women's issues" (ibid., 213). In Europe political parties tend to be more coherent than in the United States, and pressure for loyalty is strong when it comes to voting in the chamber (e.g. Lovenduski and Norris 2003). Thus, for most European countries it is necessary to use indicators that capture behavior in earlier stages of the parliamentary process.

One needs to be aware that the analyses in this chapter deal with changes that take place in a rather hidden process. Methodologically, I have tried to get indicators on what is going on in all these formal and informal meetings that make up the parliamentary world. In the Swedish parliament the voting in the chamber can be compared to the tip of an iceberg. Decisive steps are taken in many contexts – such as in the party groups and various committees – over a long period of time, and surveys are used to get a valid picture of the dynamics at work.[3]

I also want to point to the fact that the following analyses are based upon a survey question where there is nothing in the formulation that can be said to stimulate MPs to start thinking in terms of gender. This is an important point. I do not wish to arrive at answers where there is any suspicion that the respondents have adapted themselves to expectations of "femininity" or "masculinity."

Table 5.2 reports responses to the open-ended question, "Which area or areas of politics are you most interested in?" MPs could choose any area or areas, and the answers were coded using a detailed coding scheme. Included in the table are the three most frequently mentioned areas. Also included are the results from the open-ended question asked of voters about important policy areas informing their party choices (see Table 3.1).

If we look at the results for voters, it is clear that since the 1998 election, social policy has been the policy area that women have identified as most important in informing their decisions about which party to vote for. Over time, social policy becomes a top-three issue for male citizens as well. However, it is only in the 2002 election that social policy is the number one area among male voters. High on men's list we find jobs, taxes, and the economy. Women also frequently mention jobs as an important policy area, but not taxes or the economy.

If we then turn to the results for MPs, it is equally clear that social policy on all survey occasions is found on the top-three list among women. However, it is only in 2002 and 2006 that we find social policy among the three most frequently mentioned policy areas among men MPs. High on men's list we find jobs, education, and the economy. Women MPs also frequently mention jobs and education, but to a lesser extent the economy.

In sum, there are obvious overlaps between the priorities among women and men – in terms of both male and female voters and male and female elected representatives – but at the same time it is reasonable to conclude that there is a gender gap in *the emphasis* on different policy areas: More women MPs than men MPs give high priority to the area of social policy, which is a highly prioritized area among women voters; thus, this indicator shows that women MPs are less "at odds" with women voters than are their male colleagues.[4]

Variation across time and groups of MPs in priority for welfare politics

There is always a risk of theoretical definitions of women's interests getting mixed up with everyday language, "what he or she is interested in." This problem should not be overemphasized. Most theoretical concepts are hard to operationalize, and the only reasonable solution is to be careful when drawing conclusions and to strive for a variety of indicators.

The results in Figure 5.2 build on the same open-ended question to MPs that was used in Table 5.2. This time, however, all answers that refer to "social policy," "family policy," "senior citizens/elderly care," and/or "health care" are merged into one category labeled "welfare politics." There is no clear demarcation between the different policy areas discussed above, and together they can serve as a proxy for policies that, in the Swedish context, affect the conflict between work and family. Figure 5.2 shows the percentage of MPs who referred to welfare politics in the open-ended question on personal interests. The different graphs illustrate answers for all MPs, plus answers for women MPs and men MPs separately.

Table 5.2 The top three policy areas among women and men MPs and voters, 1985–2010

	Women				Men			
	MPs	%	Voters	%	MPs	%	Voters	%
2010	Jobs	27	Social policy	44	Jobs	23	Jobs	33
	Social policy	27	Education	33	Foreign policy	22	Social policy	29
	Education	20	Jobs	33	Education	20	Economy	20
2006	Jobs	30	Social policy	39	Jobs	33	Jobs	37
	Social policy	28	Jobs	32	Social policy	21	Social policy	26
	Education	28	Education	31	Education	17	Education	18
2002	Social policy	28	Social policy	54	Social policy	23	Social policy	44
	Education	26	Education	43	Education	21	Education	35
	Family policy	16	Elderly care	19	Business	18	Taxes	25
1994	Social policy	34	Jobs	39	Economy	39	Jobs	33
	Education	23	Environment	26	Jobs	24	Economy	20
	Jobs	20	Social policy	25	Foreign policy	23	Social policy	18
1988	Social policy	41	Environment	50	Economy	28	Environment	42
	Environment	26	Family policy	24	Foreign policy	27	Taxes	23
	Foreign policy	19	Social policy	18	Environment	24	Social policy	12
1985	Social policy	35	Family policy	25	Economy	40	Jobs	26
	Economy	25	Environment	23	Jobs	27	Environment	23
	Education	24	Jobs	23	Business	24	Taxes	23

(Swedish Parliamentary Surveys, Department of Political Science, University of Gothenburg). See Table 3.1 for Voters

92 *Room for women's interests and concerns*

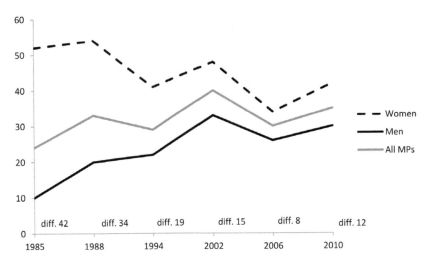

Figure 5.2 Proportion of Swedish MPs who have welfare politics as an area of personal interest, 1985–2010 (%)
The question reads: "Which area or areas of politics are you most interested in?" The question is open-ended, and respondents could choose any area or areas. The graph shows the percentages of women and men who answered social policy, family policy, senior citizens/elderly care, health care, or similar answers.
(Swedish Parliamentary Surveys, Department of Political Science, University of Gothenburg)

The first thing to note in Figure 5.2 is that between 1985 and 2010 there is a slight increase, from 24 to 35 percent, if we look at the answers among all MPs.[5] The second thing to note is that women MPs on all survey occasions give higher priority to the area of welfare politics than men MPs, but the gender gap is, over time, decreasing: in 1985 it is 42 percentage points and in 2010 the corresponding figure is 12 percentage points. It should be noted that a particularly large decrease in the gender gap, from 34 to 19 percentage points, occurs between the 1988 and 1994 election. Thus, Figure 5.2 shows a pattern that resembles the convergence previously found in the analysis of committee assignments (Figure 4.2).

Before I comment further on these results, let us turn to a multivariate regression analysis to capture more carefully variation across time and across different groups of MPs. The dependent variable in Table 5.3 is a dichotomy separating MPs mentioning welfare politics as an area of personal interest from the rest (see Figure 5.2), and the independent variables included are gender, party affiliation, age, parliamentary experience, education, and whether the MP holds a distinguished power position. The Conservative Party is, once again, used as the reference category, and in this case it is motivated by the fact that the Conservative Party used to be less supportive of a comprehensive welfare state than the other political parties in Sweden.

Table 5.3 Determinants of Swedish MPs' priorities for welfare politics as an area of personal interest, 2002, 2006, and 2010 (logistic regression)

	2002			2006			2010		
	B	SE	Sig.	B	SE	Sig.	B	SE	Sig.
Gender	0.93	0.30	0.00	0.37	0.28	0.18	0.47	0.27	0.08
Lft	0.75	0.61	0.22	0.84	0.55	0.13	0.14	0.56	0.80
SocDem	1.47	0.47	0.00	0.23	0.40	0.56	0.31	0.36	0.39
Grn	0.28	0.85	0.74	-0.46	0.81	0.57	-0.32	0.56	0.56
Cen	1.22	0.63	0.05	0.28	0.53	0.59	-0.10	0.60	0.86
Lib	-0.01	0.59	0.97	0.78	0.56	0.16	0.08	0.56	0.88
ChrDem	2.49	0.60	0.00	0.94	0.55	0.08	1.30	0.59	0.02
SweDem	n.a.	n.a.	n.a.	n.a.	n.a.	n.a.	0.57	0.75	0.44
Con (reference)									
Age	0.03	0.01	0.03	0.02	0.01	0.09	0.03	0.01	0.01
Experience	-0.05	0.03	0.10	0.00	0.03	0.78	-0.04	0.02	0.10
Education	-0.36	0.33	0.27	-0.64	0.32	0.04	0.04	0.32	0.88
Power position	0.28	0.34	0.41	-0.23	0.36	0.51	0.42	0.30	0.16
Constant	-2.96	0.90	0.00	-2.18	0.80	0.00	-2.59	0.78	0.00
Nagelkerke	0.24			0.10			0.08		

(Swedish Parliamentary Surveys, Department of Political Science, University of Gothenburg)

Included in the analysis are results for 2002, 2006, and 2010, which makes it possible to follow the most interesting shifts that take place.

In the 1980s the area of welfare politics was truly gendered in the Swedish Riksdag: women in all parties and all age groups gave higher priority to this policy area than did their male counterparts (Wängnerud 1998, 159). In the 1990s something started to happen. First of all, it can be noticed in Table 5.3 that age (measured in years) is significant in 2002, 2006, and 2010, and the results show that older MPs give higher priority to the area of welfare politics than younger MPs. In 2002 the answers from MPs within the Social Democratic Party, the Center Party, and the Christian Democratic Party are significantly different from the answers from MPs within the Conservative Party, meaning that MPs within these parties give higher priority to welfare politics than MPs within the Conservative Party. In 2006 and 2010 it is, however, only the Christian Democratic Party that is significantly different from the Conservative Party. A further item of note in Table 5.3 is that gender is significant in 2002 and 2010, but not in 2006. A more extensive analysis, including all survey occasions, shows that the effect of gender has decreased since 1985, but the effect has not gone. Thus, the most important conclusions of the analyses in this section are that differences between political parties are decreasing and that welfare politics, despite reduced gender gaps, remains a gendered area in the Riksdag.

Attitudes toward policy proposals linked to women's interests

In Sweden welfare politics are to a large extent designed to reduce the conflict between work and family; however, it is less evident that they are designed to increase personal integrity for women. By personal integrity I refer to policies that may reduce the prevalence of sexual harassment, violence, and threats.

In a comparative study of Sweden and Australia, covering the period 1960–90, Jessica Lindvert (2002) underpins the notion that in Sweden the area of gender equality is strongly focused on women as workers and includes policies that build on the redistribution of resources, such as publicly funded child care. Policies that build on recognition/justice for women, such as sex discrimination and violence against women, are not to be seen as equally established on the political agenda. Lindvert builds her analysis on official policy documents and discusses a path dependency in Sweden that leads to a focus on women as workers, whereas in Australia a corresponding path dependency leads to a focus on civil rights issues.

The Swedish Parliamentary Surveys do not include a question on attitudes toward sex discrimination or violence against women, but there is a question on attitudes toward the proposal to ban all forms of pornography, which can be seen as an indicator on standpoints related to women's integrity. Figure 5.3 includes attitudes among MPs toward four different proposals. Two proposals relate to the structure of the welfare state, a proposal to *reduce the public sector* and a proposal to *provide more health care under private management*. In addition, the survey includes two proposals that relate more clearly to the theoretical definition of women's interests, a proposal to *ban all forms of pornography*, which, as discussed above, relates to personal integrity, and a proposal to *introduce a six-hour workday for all workers*, which relates to the possibility of successfully combining work and family.

Figure 5.3 shows attitudes among male and female voters (thin lines) and male and female MPs (thick lines). Dotted lines represent attitudes among men, and solid lines, attitudes among women. Percentages represent the number answering "very good" or "fairly good" – that is, the number supporting each alternative. The attitudes among male and female voters have previously been reported in Figure 3.2.

In Chapter 3 it was found that the two proposals measuring attitudes toward the structure of the welfare state – to reduce the public sector and to provide more health care under private management – display comparatively small gender gaps. This is true for the level of voters but also for the level of MPs. What is most remarkable about these two proposals is that, over time, voters are becoming less supportive than MPs. Since the election of 2002 male and female MPs are, on average, displaying more positive attitudes than the average

Room for women's interests and concerns   95

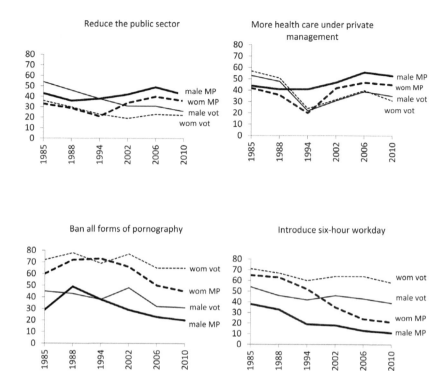

Figure 5.3 Proportion of Swedish MPs and voters who support specific proposals, 1985–2010 (%)
(Swedish Parliamentary Surveys and Election Studies (see Figure 3.2), Department of Political Science, University of Gothenburg)

male and female voter. As noted, gender gaps are not big, but still the results in Figure 5.3 show that women voters comprise the group displaying the least positive attitudes toward the proposal to reduce the public sector.

The next item of note is the results for the two proposals that more clearly relate to women's interests, to ban all forms of pornography and to introduce a six-hour workday. The results in Figure 5.3 visualize that there is a distinct gender gap in attitudes toward the proposal to ban all forms of pornography. Women voters make up the group most in favor of this proposal, and the second, displaying comparatively positive attitudes, is that of women MPs. However, at the same time it should be noticed that there is a downward trend among women MPs: in 1985 60 percent of women MPs supported the proposal to ban all forms of pornography; in 2010 the corresponding figure is 45 percent. The downward trend among women MPs is even clearer if we look at the proposal to introduce a six-hour workday. In 1985 65 percent among women MPs supported this proposal; in 2010 the corresponding figure is 21 percent. If we look at the results for the proposal to introduce a six-hour workday, it is obvious that women MPs have gradually moved toward men MPs in their opinions. Among women voters, however, the support for the proposal to introduce a six-hour workday remains remarkably high and stable.

Results from a multivariate regression analysis (not displayed in a table) of the answers from MPs show that attitudes toward the proposals to reduce the public sector and to provide more health care under private management are for the most part explained by MPs' placement on the ideological left–right scale (MPs to the right are most supportive). The multivariate regression confirms that MPs' gender has never played any significant role in these matters.

A further result from the multivariate regression is that when it comes to the proposal to ban all forms of pornography, the effect of gender is significant on all survey occasions – more women MPs than men MPs are in favor of this proposal – but party affiliation also plays an important role. MPs from the Conservative Party are less supportive of this proposal than other MPs, as are, on most survey occasions, MPs from the Liberal Party. As displayed in Figure 5.3, the most dramatic change taking place concerns the support for the proposal to introduce a six-hour workday. In the multivariate regression analysis gender remains significant up to 2002, but in 2006 and 2010 there is no significant effect of gender; it is instead MPs' placement on the left–right scale that can explain variation on these occasions (MPs to the left are more positive about the proposal).

Taken together, the results so far are pretty mixed; on the one hand, it is fair to say that women MPs remain less "at odds" with women citizens than men MPs, but on the other hand, there are quite substantial changes taking place. Welfare politics are, without doubt, high on the political agenda in the Riksdag. Since 1985 the number of men MPs who give priority to this policy area has increased, and in this case it may be accurate to talk about a "spillover effect" from women MPs. However, when we look at the results from the analysis on attitudes toward the proposals that are most in line with the theoretical definition of women's interests, the result is quite the opposite; there seems to be a "spillover effect" from male to female MPs. These results point to complex dynamics at work between the room available for women's interests and concerns and the solutions favored once an issue is on the table.

The role of group awareness

The core mechanism at work in the theory of the politics of presence can be likened, as stated previously, to an invisible hand; female politicians are expected to be better equipped to represent the interests of female voters, because they, at least to some extent, share the same experiences. Before we reach the final conclusion of this chapter we shall look at an alternative way of analyzing the developments taking place. In the writings of Iris Marion Young there is an emphasis on *intentionality*; to represent women – or any other disadvantaged group in society – politicians must be explicitly aware of the social position of that group. I have used the label "the politics of awareness" to distinguish the ideas brought forward by Young (2000) from the ideas brought forward by Phillips (1995).

Chapter 2 contained an analysis of "self-defined champions" of women's interests. The question concerned how important it is to MPs, personally, to promote women's interests and concerns. Self-defined champions of women's interests were assumed to believe that it is *very important* to promote women's interests and concerns. In the following analysis "self-defined champion" is to be seen as an independent variable. The results are used to construct two different categories: MPs considered being strong versus weak feminists.

The following analyses focus on four dichotomous dependent variables that have appeared previously in this chapter: (i) a dichotomy that distinguishes MPs who give priority to gender equality (Figure 5.1) from the rest; (ii) a dichotomy that distinguishes MPs who give priority to welfare politics (Figure 5.2) from the rest; (iii) a dichotomy that distinguishes MPs who support the proposal to introduce a six-hour workday (Figure 5.3) from the rest; and finally (iv) a dichotomy that distinguishes MPs who support the proposal to ban all forms of pornography (Figure 5.3) from the rest.

The analysis presented in Figure 5.4 suggests an interesting tendency: over time, feminist commitment becomes more and more important as an explanatory factor. For the indicator showing priority for the policy area of gender equality, the result is quite clear: it is women MPs considered strong feminists who give priority to this area. For the indicator showing priority for the policy area of welfare politics, the result displayed in Figure 5.4 is more complex: In 1985 gender, regardless of feminist commitment, is the most significant factor. In 1994 priority for welfare politics is spread quite evenly across all groups, and then in 2010 it is women MPs considered strong feminists who give highest priority to this policy area. A path analysis confirms that the link between being a female self-defined champion of women's interests and the priority given to welfare politics over time becomes more evident. In 1985 there was a strong direct effect of gender on the priority for welfare politics, but in 2010 the effect of gender was to a large extent transmitted through the factor of being a self-defined champion.

If we then turn to the results in Figure 5.4 for the analyses on attitudes toward the proposals to introduce a six-hour workday and to ban all forms of pornography, it can be noted that in 1994 and 2010 men MPs considered strong feminists are more positive in their attitudes than women MPs considered weak feminists. This pattern does not emerge in 1985 when women MPs, regardless of their feminist commitments, are more positive in their attitudes than men MPs. If we look at the results for the proposal to introduce a six-hour workday, the results for 2010 show that men MPs considered strong feminists actually display the most positive attitudes.

98 Room for women's interests and concerns

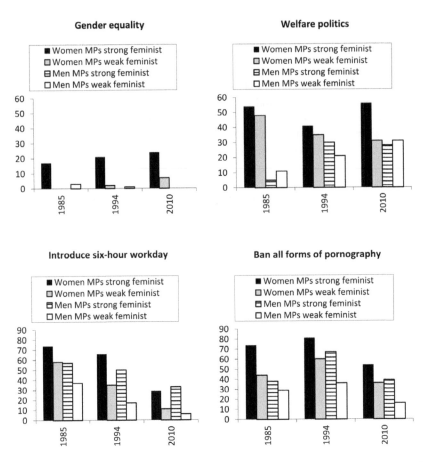

Figure 5.4 Gender equality and welfare politics as areas of personal interest and attitudes toward the proposals to ban all forms of pornography and introduce a six-hour workday among MPs considered strong versus weak feminists, 1985, 1994, and 2010 (%)

Strong feminist refers to members of parliament who consider the duty to promote women's interests and concerns "very important"; weak feminist refers to those who consider this duty as "fairly important," "not very important," or "not at all important" (categories are merged). For more information see Figure 3.2.
(Swedish Parliamentary Surveys, Department of Political Science, University of Gothenburg)

All in all, the interpretation I make is that the theory of the politics of presence becomes increasingly inadequate as the sole explanatory theme when it comes to the room available for women's interests and concerns. Important to note is that the relevant counterhypotheses do not only concern ideology or party affiliation. It is becoming increasingly more important to take into account the theory of the politics of awareness.

Acting in the interests of women?

So far, the main indicators used in this chapter have focused on MPs' priorities and attitudes. These measures have been presented as indicators of activities going on in early stages of the parliamentary process. Before we reach the concluding discussion we shall look at an indicator more directly linked to behavior. In 2010 the Swedish Parliamentary Survey included a question on how often MPs have contacted a cabinet minister to put forward demands of women/women's organizations. Figure 5.5 presents the percentages reporting that at least once, during the past year, they have personally contacted a cabinet minister on behalf of women.

The results in Figure 5.5 to a large extent confirm the conclusions in the previous section: yes, gender is important to take into account; more women MPs than men MPs report contact with a cabinet minister on behalf of women. However, even more important to consider is whether an MP is a self-defined champion of women's interests or not; it is self-defined champions who report the most frequent contact on behalf of women (cf. Esaiasson 2000).

The room available versus direction

It goes without saying that parliaments are complex institutions and that it is a methodological challenge to test empirically the assumptions brought forward in the theory of the politics of presence or, for that matter, the theory of the politics of awareness. Karen Beckwith (2007), among others,

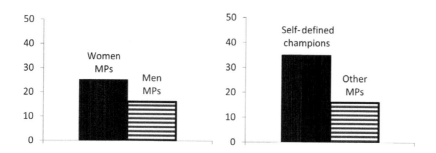

Figure 5.5 Acting in the interests of women
The question reads: "During the past year, how often have you personally contacted cabinet ministers to put forward preferences of women/women's organizations?" The response alternatives were: "at least once a month," "sometimes," and "never." Included here is the percentage answering "at least once a month" or "sometimes."
(Swedish Parliamentary Surveys, Department of Political Science, University of Gothenburg, 2010)

has suggested that studies in this field ought to be longitudinal in design; we should follow what happens "from the start," when women are few, up to the point when women are present in large numbers. Longitudinal designs of this kind are hard to conduct. The research strategy in this chapter has been to use several different indicators in cross-sectional analysis and to include control variables to isolate effects of gender.

One of the most important conclusions of this chapter, and also of the previous chapter on internal parliamentary working procedures, is how important it is to include many time points in the analyses: the results for 1985 are very different from the results of 2010. However, taking a bird's-eye view of the results, I find that the major change is not about the size of the gender gap but about a shift in the driving forces at work. Over time it seems to be more and more important to have self-defined champions of women's interests in the parliament. However, at the same time more women MPs than men MPs are self-defined champions of women's interests, so the theory of the politics of awareness should not, in any simplistic way, be put up against the theory of the politics of presence.

If we compare 1985 and 2010, the results presented in this chapter point to an increase in the room available on the political agenda for welfare politics. For gender-equality policies the picture emerging is more of a "plateau" or stabilization in the latter part of the period studied. There is no clear sign that the emergence of two distinct ideological blocs in the Riksdag (see Figure 2.2) – a left-green bloc and a center-right bloc – has had an effect on the room available for women's interests and concerns. We know that important real-world changes have been taking place in Sweden during recent decades, with increased marketization of the public sector. Thus a reasonable interpretation is that the social democratic welfare state has been challenged by a liberal, market-based welfare state. By extension, this means that the number of policy alternatives available in this area has increased.

Currently, Swedish voters are more skeptical about proposals such as those to reduce the public sector and provide more health care under private management than they were in the 1980s. Changes of opinion have led to a situation where MPs are more positive toward these proposals than voters, which was not the case in the 1980s. In these shifts, gender is not a decisive factor. However, when we talk about changes of opinion connected to proposals such as banning all forms of pornography and introducing a six-hour workday, gender is, at least in reference to voters, very important to take into account.

How should the results for the proposal to introduce a six-hour workday be interpreted? In the Riksdag this proposal has, over time, become even more clearly linked to the ideological left–right dimension. In practice it is the Left Party and the Green Party that currently embrace the idea of a six-hour workday. At the same time left-green parties strive for legislation guaranteeing the right to full-time employment for women in the public sector. I believe that the support among women voters for the proposal to introduce a six-hour workday indicates that the work–family conflict has not found any "proper" solution, even in the context of a Scandinavian welfare state.[6] However, this does not necessarily mean that the introduction of a six-hour workday is the only possible solution to this conflict.[7]

Finally, these results lead me to the conclusion that the definition of women's interests suggested previously in this book needs to be revised. Self-determination for women is not only about having policy alternatives to choose between, but also about the implementation of policies that change the position of women vis-à-vis men. The revision of core concepts is, however, a task for the final chapter of this book, and before we get there, we need to analyze the production of gender-sensitive legislation.

Notes

1 In research on descriptive representation of women there is a distinct, easily calculated dependent variable: What is to be explained is the numerical distribution of seats between women and men. Comparisons are made across countries and across time. Comparisons are also made between subnational units, such as between different parties or local legislatures. Research on substantive representation is less mature. This is partly because there used to be very few countries with any substantial number of women elected. However, a further complexity has to do with the fact that the dependent variable is more multifaceted. It is not self-evident what aspect an increased number of women elected will most affect, and in practice, researchers end up with a variety of solutions which make cross-country comparisons problematic.
2 OECD data are published on the website stats.oecd.org/Index.aspx?DataSetCode= SOCX_AGG.
3 In research on political representation it is quite common to rely on questionnaires and to build conclusions on indicators of attitudes, priorities, and policy promotion. For Sweden and the other Nordic countries see Esaiasson and Holmberg (1996) and Esaiasson and Heidar (2000), and for studies on Western democracies, see Miller et al. (1999).
4 Research in Sweden indicates that women MPs are more in line with attitudes and priorities among women citizens than men MPs; similarly, men MPs are more in line with attitudes and priorities among men citizens than women MPs (Oskarson and Wängnerud 1995, 1996).
5 The highest percentage, 40 percent, is found in 2002, but the second highest proportion is actually found in 2010.
6 The Labor Force Service in 2011 reported that the most common reason for women to work part time is that they cannot find suitable full-time work. The second most common reason for women to work part time is care of children (reported in *Women and Men in Sweden. Facts and Figures*, 2012, 56).
7 It should be noted that no other survey questions related to this topic were included in the Swedish Parliamentary Survey. Therefore, it is impossible to say what women citizens prefer the most when faced with different options.

Bibliography

Beckwith, Karen. 2007. "Numbers and Newness: The Descriptive and Substantive Representation of Women." *Canadian Journal of Political Science* 40(1): 27–49.

Bolzendahl, Catherine. 2014. "Opportunities and Expectations: The Gendered Organization of Legislative Committees in Germany, Sweden, and the United States." *Gender & Society*, published online August 1, 2014.

Celis, Karen, Sarah Childs, Johanna E. Kantola and Mona Lena Krook. 2014. "Constituting Women's Interests through Representative Claims." *Politics & Gender* 10(2): 149–174.

Esaiasson, Peter. 2000. "How Members of Parliament Define their Task." In *Beyond Westminster and Congress: The Nordic Experience*, ed. Peter Esaiasson and Knut Heidar. Columbus: Ohio State University Press.

Esaiasson, Peter and Knut Heidar, eds. 2000. *Beyond Westminster and Congress: The Nordic Experience*. Columbus: Ohio State University Press.

Esaiasson, Peter and Sören Holmberg. 1996. *Representation from Above. Members of Parliament and Representative Democracy in Sweden*. Aldershot: Dartmouth.

Grey, Sandra. 2006. "Numbers and Beyond: The Relevance of Critical Mass in Gender Research." *Politics & Gender* 2(4): 492–502.

Hawkesworth, Mary. 2005. "Engendering Political Science: An Immodest Proposal." *Politics & Gender* 1: 141–156.

Jeydal, Alana and Andrew J. Taylor. 2003. "Are Women Legislators Less Effective? Evidence from the U.S. House in the 103rd–105th Congress." *Political Research Quarterly* 56(1): 19–27.

Krook, Mona Lena and Fiona Mackay, eds. 2010. *Gender, Politics and Institutions: Towards a Feminist Intuitionalism*. Basingstoke and New York: Palgrave Macmillan.

Lindvert, Jessica. 2002. *Feminism som politik. Sverige och Australien 1960–1990*. Umeå: Boréa.

Lovenduski, Joni and Pippa Norris. 2003. "Westminster Women: The Politics of Presence." *Political Studies* 51(1): 84–102.

McBride, Dorothy E. and Amy G. Mazur. 2010. *The Politics of State Feminism: Innovation in Comparative Research*. Philadelphia, PA: Temple University Press.

Miller, Warren E. et al. 1999. *Policy Representation in Western Democracies*. Oxford: Oxford University Press.

Norris, Pippa. 2005. *Radical Right: Voters and Parties on the Electoral Market*. Cambridge: Cambridge University Press.

Oskarson, Maria and Lena Wängnerud. 1995. *Kvinnor som väljare och valda. Om betydelsen av kön i svensk politik*. Lund: Studentlitteratur.

Oskarson, Maria and Lena Wängnerud. 1996. "Vem representerar kvinnorna?" In *Vetenskapen om politik. Festskrift till professor emeritus Jörgen Westerståhl*, ed. Bo Rothstein and Bo Särlvik. Gothenburg: University of Gothenburg.

Oskarson, Maria and Lena Wängnerud. 2013. "The Story of the Gender Gap in Swedish Politics: Only Partially Diminishing Differences." In *Stepping Stones: Research on Political Representation, Voting Behavior, and Quality of Government*, ed. Stefan Dahlberg, Henrik Oscarsson and Lena Wängnerud. Gothenburg: University of Gothenburg.

Phillips, Anne. 1995. *The Politics of Presence*. Oxford: Oxford University Press.

Phillips, Anne. 2007. *Multiculturalism Without Culture*. Princeton, NJ: Princeton University Press.

Pitkin, Hanna F.. 1967. *The Concept of Representation*. Berkeley: University of California Press.

Rosenbluth, Frances, Rob Salmond and Michael E. Thies. 2006. "Welfare Works: Explaining Female Legislative Representation." *Politics & Gender* 2: 165–192.

Saward, Michael. 2010. *The Representative Claim*. Oxford: Oxford University Press.

Skjeie, Hege. 1992. *Den politiske betydningen av kjønn. En studie av norsk topp-politikk*. Rapport 92:11. PhD diss.. Oslo: Inst. Samfunnsforskning.

Svallfors, Stefan. 2011. "A Bedrock of Support? Trends in Welfare State Attitudes in Sweden, 1981–2010." *Social Policy & Administration* 45(7): 806–825.

Vega, Arturo and Juanita M. Firestone. 1995. "The Effects of Gender on Congressional Behavior and the Substantive Representation of Women." *Legislative Studies Quarterly* 20(2): 213–222.

Wängnerud, Lena. 1998. *Politikens andra sida. Om kvinnorepresentation i Sveriges Riksdag*. PhD diss.. Gothenburg: University of Gothenburg.

Wängnerud, Lena. 2009. "Women in Parliaments: Descriptive and Substantive Representation." *Annual Review of Political Science* 12: 51–69.

Young, Iris M. 2000. *Inclusion and Democracy*. Oxford: Oxford University Press.

6 The production of gender-sensitive legislation

"Are there concrete issues about which you believe your party's position has changed due to higher women's representation?" The question was asked of members of the Swedish Riksdag in 1994 and 2006.[1] The vast majority agreed that there were issues that had changed due to higher women's representation, and they could also specify, in answer to an open-ended question, the issues they were thinking of. In 1994 the three most frequently mentioned areas were gender equality, family policy, and social policy. In 2006 the three most frequently mentioned areas were gender equality, family policy, and violence against women.

In this chapter we shall put the claims made by Swedish MPs in perspective. The focus is on the production of gender-sensitive legislation, but the main objective is to analyze transformations in Sweden from a comparative perspective. Is it reasonable to believe that the Swedish parliament has played a role in transformations in Swedish society? More specifically, is it reasonable to believe that change in the composition of the parliament – that is, the increased number of women elected – has played a role?

The chapter consists of three parts: In the first part Swedish gender-equality policy is analyzed, and legislation which has been officially presented as "gender sensitive" will be discussed.[2] This section employs a long-term perspective, since current legislation cannot be understood without an historical context. In the second part we shall move to the subnational level in Sweden. Analyses at the subnational level facilitate a rather strict test of the link between the number of women elected and outcomes in the everyday lives of citizens. The proportion of women elected to local councils in Sweden varies considerably; in 2010 the range was from 29 to 58 percent, and this is also the case if we look at gender equality among citizens. This situation provides fertile ground for delving into matters of driving forces in gender-equality processes.

In the third part of the chapter we shall turn to the global arena. Several international organizations, such as the World Economic Forum and Social Watch, produce indices measuring gender equality in the everyday lives of citizens.[3] While we shall look at the ranking of Sweden in these lists, even more important is the employment of a multivariate analysis including a wide range of countries: if one takes into account factors such as economic development and level of democracy, is it then reasonable to believe that the proportion of women elected to parliament has an effect on the everyday lives of citizens?

It has previously been announced that this chapter on gender-sensitive legislation will be a bit more "impressionistic" than other chapters in this book, since good data on gender-sensitive legislation are scarce. However, the different parts together will shed light on the link between descriptive and substantive representation – that is, the expectation that the proportion of women elected affects the political agenda, and by extension, the everyday lives of citizens. Before we get to the different parts outlined above, we shall return to the statement in Chapter 3 that gender equality is about the capability of people to realize their potential as human beings.

The principle of each person's capability

The United Nations stresses that human development has to do with the opportunity for people to realize their potential as human beings. The UN states that real opportunity is about having real choices – that is, choices that come with "a sufficient income, an education, good health and living in a country that is not governed by tyranny."[4]

The UN bases its definition of human development on Aristotle and later philosophers like John Stuart Mill and Amartya Sen. More crucial, however, for the analysis in this chapter are the extensions made by Martha Nussbaum in her seminal book *Women and Human Development: The Capabilities Approach*, from 2000.[5] Nussbaum recognizes that there may be different obstacles hindering human development among women and men. Nussbaum (2000) argues that any definition of human development needs to build on a principle of each person's capability to develop; in many parts of the world an obstacle facing women is that they are not treated as individuals but as members of a family.

Nussbaum employs a global perspective in her analysis. She argues for a threshold level of capabilities "beneath which it is held that truly human functioning is not available for citizens" (Nussbaum 2000, 6). In Sweden and most Western democracies, women have passed that threshold. In fact, most legislation that recognizes women as individuals, rather than as members of a family, was in place as early as the 1960s in Sweden. Thus, the 1970s and 1980s were periods when legislation was directed toward accelerating gender-equality processes.

Georgina Waylen is another prominent scholar who employs a global perspective in her analysis on hindering and enabling factors in processes related to gender equality. In *Engendering Transitions: Women's Mobilization, Institutions, and Gender Outcomes*, Waylen (2007) analyzes East-Central Europe, Latin America, and South Africa in transitions to democracy. What we can learn from her study is that change – that is, a strengthened position for women – is easier to achieve in the least contested policy areas. Waylen notices comparatively far-reaching changes in the regulation of marriage, but fewer changes in the area of reproductive rights/abortion (ibid., 2007, 202). What counts as a contested area is, however, context dependent. In a Protestant, secular country like Sweden, reproductive rights/abortion is no longer a contested area. The following analysis will show a sequencing of gender-sensitive legislation in Sweden where policies targeting women have gradually been replaced by gender-equality policies targeting men.

Swedish gender-equality policy

The 1995 UN Fourth World Conference on Women in Beijing endorsed gender mainstreaming as critical to achieving gender equality.[6] Gender mainstreaming clearly permeates contemporary Swedish gender-equality policy, where the overall objective is to "ensure that women and men have equal power to shape society and their own lives." Table 6.1 shows the four areas that are seen as most important for achieving that goal: an equal distribution of power and influence, economic equality between women and men; equal distribution of unpaid care and household work; and finally, an end to men's violence against women.

The official gender-equality policy presented in Table 6.1 includes two areas that are more closely linked to changing behavior among women – namely, the goal of an equal distribution of power and influence, and the goal of economic equality between women and men. Two areas are more closely linked to changing behavior among men – namely, the goal of an equal distribution of unpaid care and household work, and the goal of an end to men's violence against women. Thus, gender-equality policies in Sweden target not only women as a group, but also men as a group.

It should be noted that the policy presented in Table 6.1 is, with one exception, formulated in gender-neutral language. The interpretation that some areas are linked to a changing behavior among women, and others to changing behavior among men, builds on facts and figures on citizens' everyday lives, which, for example, show that most unpaid care and household work is carried out by women.[7] Thus, to achieve equal distribution, men need to increase their participation in this area. The only time that the policy in Table 6.1 refers to a specific gendered situation is in stating the objective of "an end to men's violence against women."

Table 6.1 shows that gender mainstreaming is expected to touch "all areas of society." What can also be seen in Table 6.1 is that gender equality is supposed to be implemented by all government agencies: there is a minister for gender equality, but each minister is responsible for gender equality in his/her area.[8] In addition, every county administrative board is supposed to have its own expert in gender equality. Let us now consider a long-term perspective that shows how gender-sensitive legislation has developed in Sweden since the mid-1800s.

Table 6.1 Official definition and national coordination of gender equality in Sweden

Swedish gender-equality policy	National coordination of gender-equality work
The overall objective for gender-equality policy is to ensure that women and men have equal power to shape society and their own lives. Among other things, this implies the following: • An equal distribution of power and influence: women and men shall have the same rights and opportunities to be active citizens and to be able to form the terms for decision making. • Economic equality between women and men: women and men shall have the same opportunities and conditions with regard to education and paid work that provide them with the means to achieve lifelong economic independence. • Equal distribution of unpaid care and household work: women and men shall take the same responsibility for household work and shall have the same opportunities to give and receive care on equal terms. • An end to men's violence against women: women and men, girls and boys shall have equal rights and opportunities in terms of physical integrity. • Gender equality concerns all areas of society: to achieve gender equality in society, is it necessary to have a gender-equality perspective in all areas. This strategy is called gender mainstreaming. This means that analyses of women's and men's, girls' and boys' situations and conditions shall be included in decision-making data, and that the consequences of proposals are analyzed with consideration to gender equality among women and men. Gender mainstreaming is based on the understanding that gender equality is created where the resources are distributed and decisions are made. Therefore, a gender-equality perspective must be incorporated in all decision making by the actors who normally take part in decision making.	The minister for gender equality coordinates the policies of gender equality in the government. Each minister is responsible for gender equality in her/his policy area. The Division for Gender Equality is responsible, under the minister for gender equality, for coordination of the government's work on gender equality, special gender-equality initiatives, and development of methods to implement the government's gender-equality policy. There are experts in *gender-equality issues* at every county administrative board. The equality ombudsperson sees that antidiscrimination legislation and the Parental Leave Act are followed. There is a council against discrimination that can impose fines on employers and educators if they do not take active measures to prevent discrimination, such as discrimination on grounds of sex.

(Adapted from Statistics Sweden. Women and Men in Sweden: Facts and Figures, 2012)

Gender-sensitive legislation in Sweden: A long-term perspective

It is a delicate matter where to begin when describing developments within a certain policy area such as gender equality. The following description starts in 1842 with the introduction of compulsory elementary education for boys and girls in Sweden. One can expect that this law had a strong signal effect: boys and girls were to be treated equally.[9] The list in Table 6.2 illustrates that compulsory elementary school was introduced in an era when few adult women had economic or political rights. Table 6.2 includes gender-sensitive legislation in Sweden 1842–1970, divided into two periods: 1842–1921 (that is, before women gain suffrage), and 1922–70 (that is, after political rights are introduced but before women enter the Riksdag in large numbers).[10]

This is a simplification, but the period 1842–1921 can be described as a period when women in Sweden gained economic and political rights (Rönnbäck 2004). For example, in 1874 married women gained the right to control their own incomes, and in 1921 national suffrage was introduced. What can be seen in Table 6.2 is that, on the whole, unmarried women gained legal rights before married women. This indicates that women, once married, were at that time seen as individuals to a lesser degree than other adult citizens (cf. Nussbaum 2000).

During the period 1922–70 the individualization of married women is a major theme in Swedish gender-equality policies. For example, in 1939 it was enshrined in law that gainfully employed women may not be dismissed due to pregnancy, childbirth, or marriage. Moreover, in 1951 women were entitled to retain their Swedish citizenship upon marriage to foreign citizens. An important step in the individualization of married women was the separate income tax assessment for wife and husband that was introduced in 1971 (see Table 6.3).

The period 1922–70 is also characterized by the introduction of laws/regulations pertaining to women as workers. For example, in 1955 three months' paid maternity leave for working women on the birth of a child was introduced, and in 1960 employers and unions agreed to abolish the separate wage rate that had previously put women in a disadvantaged position. In addition, the list included in Table 6.2 shows that reproductive rights were approved comparatively early in Sweden: in 1938 contraception was legalized, in 1964 the birth control pill was approved, and in 1975 (see Table 6.3) a new abortion law, which gave women the right to decide up to the eighteenth week, was approved.

It should be noted that the policies included in Table 6.2 represent changes taking place over a period of more than 100 years. The list underpins the notion that policies strengthening the position of women were in place before women started to enter the Riksdag in large numbers. In conclusion, this means that for some changes to take place it is not necessary to have a high number of women elected. In 1970 the number of women in the Riksdag was 14 percent, and only two out of 19 cabinet ministers were women (Bergqvist et al. 2000).

Table 6.2 Gender-sensitive legislation, 1842–1970

Period 1842–1921	Period 1922–70
1842 Compulsory elementary school introduced for boys and girls	1925 With some exceptions, women gain the same right as men to civil service jobs
1845 Equal inheritance rights guaranteed for women and men	1927 Public upper-secondary schools opened to girls
1846 Widows, divorcees, and unmarried women entitled to work in manual trades and some commerce	1931 Maternity insurance benefits introduced
1858 Unmarried women over 25 years of age able to attain majority by court order. Marriage means a return to minority status	1935 Equal basic pensions adopted for women and men
1859 Women entitled to some teaching positions	1938 Contraception legalized. Child support assistance established. Financial assistance to mothers established. Universal maternity allowance established
1863 Unmarried women attain majority at the age of 25	
1864 Husbands lose legal right to strike their wives	
1870 Women gain right to take high school diploma at private schools	1939 Gainfully employed women cannot be dismissed due to pregnancy, childbirth, or marriage
1873 Women gain right to take degrees with some exceptions (doctorates in law and theology)	1947 Equal pay for equal work guaranteed for state employees. Child allowances introduced
1874 Married women gain right to control their own incomes	1950 Both parents declared a child's legal guardians
1884 Unmarried women attain majority at the age of 21	1951 Women entitled to retain their Swedish citizenship upon marriage to foreign citizens
1901 Women gain right to four weeks' unpaid maternity leave	1955 Three months' paid maternity leave for working women on birth of child
1919 All women gain suffrage for municipal elections and the right to hold office at municipal and county levels	1958 Women entitled to be ordained as clergy
	1960 Employers and unions agree to abolish separate wage rates for women within a five-year period
1921 Women gain national suffrage and the right to hold office at the national level. Married women attain majority at the age of 21. The new marriage code gives wives and husbands equal legal status	1964 Use of birth control pill approved
	1965 Rape within marriage criminalized
	1969 Compulsory schools adopt new curriculum, and are encouraged to promote equal opportunities
	1970 Secondary schools adopt new curriculum, and are encouraged to promote equal opportunities

(Adapted from Statistics Sweden. Women and Men in Sweden: Facts and Figures, 2012)

Table 6.3 includes gender-sensitive legislation in 1971–2011, divided into two periods: 1971–85, and 1986–2011. In 1985 the number of women in the Riksdag passed the threshold of 30 percent (see Figure 2.1). In current research on women, gender, and politics the concept of "critical mass" is intensely debated. Some scholars seek to identify a threshold number – a "tipping point" – at which the impact of women's presence in parliaments becomes apparent; in these debates a figure of about 30 percent is often mentioned. However, others criticize the concept of critical mass as being too mechanical and implying immediate change at a certain level. They focus instead on "critical acts" (Dahlerup 1988) to explore the questions of who is pushing for change consistent with women's interests, and what kinds of strategies are useful (Dahlerup 2006; Childs and Krook 2006). The cut-off point of 1985 in Table 6.3 may give a hint of the relevance of a critical mass perspective.

The previous list (Table 6.2) shows that the first policies aimed at accelerating gender-equality processes were introduced in the late 1960s. In 1969 compulsory schools adopted a new curriculum in which schools were encouraged to promote equal opportunities; in 1970 a similar policy was introduced into the curriculum of secondary schools. During the 1970s policies aimed at accelerating gender-equality processes were extended to the labor market. For example, in 1976 an ordinance for equal opportunities in civil service was approved.

The year 1974 was a landmark in Swedish gender-equality policy, when parents became entitled to share parental allowances upon the birth of a child; the previous legislation targeted mothers alone. Sofie Cedstrand (2011) shows that an idea bearing on this legislation was that the new policy would contribute to changes in sex roles – in people's understandings of femininity and masculinity – but the law was also seen as realpolitik that would get more women into the workforce.

The law in 1974 was a landmark, because it explicitly aimed to bring men into a traditionally female sphere – that is, increasing fathers' share in the care of small children. The list in Table 6.3 shows that in the period 1986–2011 policies targeting the behavior of men become relatively common. In 1995 the "Daddy month" was introduced; the new law said that at least one month of parental leave must be used by the mother and one by the father; in 2002 this was extended to 60 days of parental leave reserved for each parent (days that cannot be transferred). Over time the number of days has increased, and currently parental leave allowance covers 480 days, which is about 16 months.[11]

The list in Table 6.3 also shows that during the period 1986–2011 policies targeting men's behavior also covered the areas of violence against women and the purchase of sexual services. In 1999 a much-debated law prohibiting the purchase of sexual services, a practice more common among men than women, was approved. However, the sale of sexual services, a practice more common among women than men, was not banned (Erikson 2011; Jakobsson and Kotsadam 2013).

Table 6.3 Gender-sensitive legislation, 1971–2011

Period 1971–85	Period 1986–2011
1971 Separate income tax assessment for wife and husband introduced	**1987** New Cohabitation Act governs joint property of cohabiting couples (unmarried)
1974 Parents entitled to share parental allowances upon the birth of a child	**1988** National five-year plan of action initiated to promote equal opportunities
1975 Under new abortion law a woman has the right to decide until the eighteenth week	**1992** New Equal Opportunities Act brought into effect
1976 Equal opportunities mandated in civil service. Persons aged 25 years and over gain right to decide under Sterilization Act	**1994** Equal Opportunities Act revised to reflect new national policy for equal opportunities. Gender statistics made part of Sweden's official statistics
1977 Agreement made between employers and unions on equal opportunities	**1995** Registered Partnership Act. New regulation states that at least one month of parental leave must be used by mother and one by father
1979 Right to six-hour workday instituted for parents of small children	
1980 Law enacted against sex discrimination in employment. Spousal means test for student loan abolished. Equal opportunities agreement reached with municipal and county governments. Compulsory schools adopt new curriculum and are now required to promote equal opportunities. Under new law on succession to the throne, monarch's firstborn daughter or son succeeds to the throne	**1998** Penal Code amended by Act on Violence against Women. Act on Prohibition against Female Genital Mutilation passed. Equal Opportunities Act tightened concerning sexual harassment
	1999 Law passed prohibiting the purchase of sexual services
	2000 National Council for Peace for Women founded
1982 New laws ban pornographic "live shows" in places open to the public, provide social security points for care in home of children under three years of age, and ensure public funding of women's organizations. New name-change law allows couples, at time of marriage, to decide which name they will use	**2001** A more stringent version of the Equal Opportunities Act comes into force
	2002 Number of days of parental leave increased by 30; sickness benefit increased to 480 days, 60 of which are reserved for each parent and cannot be transferred
	2003 Change in law on ban of visitation rights extends the ban such that it can also apply to the joint home
1983 New equal opportunities agreement reached between employers and unions. All occupations opened to women, including armed forces	**2004** Government adopts a strategy for gender mainstreaming in government offices
1984 State Sector Equal Opportunities Ordinance passed	**2005** New legislation on sexual crimes passed
1985 Equal opportunities agreement instituted for public companies/utilities	

112 *The production of gender-sensitive legislation*

Period 1971–85	Period 1986–2011
	2009 Discrimination Act enters into force to combat, among other things, discrimination on grounds of gender and of transgender identity or expression. Equal Opportunities Act ceases. A new agency, the Equality Ombudsperson, is formed, and the equal opportunities ombudsperson ceases. Gender-neutral marriage law enacted
	2011 Sweden signs the Council of Europe Convention on preventing and combating violence against women and domestic violence

(Adapted from Statistics Sweden. Women and Men in Sweden: Facts and Figures, 2012)

Actors driving change?

In the introduction to this chapter I referred to the question asked of Swedish MPs on two occasions: "Are there concrete issues about which you believe your party's position has changed due to higher women's representation?" The results showed that the vast majority believe there are issues that have changed due to higher women's representation. The issues most frequently mentioned, in 1994, were gender equality, family policy, and social policy. In 2006 the most frequently mentioned issues were gender equality, family policy, and violence against women. The results in the previous section substantiate the finding that, over time, violence against women is becoming a more prominent area in Swedish politics.

To reach a final evaluation of the claims made by Swedish MPs, one needs to do case studies tracing actors driving change in all the different areas listed in Tables 6.2 and 6.3. How else are we supposed to know whether women representatives have been significant actors? Erikson (2011) provides an example of an in-depth study on the Swedish Sex Purchase Act from 1999. She shows that women in non-parliamentary organizations initially were the main actors driving change and that at later stages women in the Riksdag became important allies.

Case studies in different areas related to gender equality in Sweden tend to confirm the pattern displayed in Chapter 5 of this book: there is a difference in emphasis with more women than men MPs giving priority to policies strengthening the position of women (Cedstrand 2011; Freidenvall 2006; Hirdman 2014; Karlsson 1996; Sainsbury 1993). However, to succeed in the parliamentary process, women MPs need to find allies among men. Comparisons with other countries indicate that the development in Sweden should not be taken for granted. Cedstrand (2011) compares parental leave legislation in Sweden and Denmark, and she shows that, in the 1970s,

Denmark chose a different route and continued with policies targeting women/mothers. Lindvert (2002) compares gender-equality policy in Sweden and Australia in 1960–90, and shows that policies strengthening women's position in the workforce are much more prevalent in the Swedish than in the Australian case.

The great advantage of case studies, using process tracing, is that they can display friction between actors and positions abandoned along the way. For example, the women's branch of the Social Democratic Party in Sweden favor shared parental leave – that is, an equal number of nontransferable days for mothers and fathers – but so far, they have not managed to convince the entire party to adopt this proposal.[12] The disadvantage of case studies of this kind is that it is hard to include a large number of control variables to test the impact of different actors. There may, for example, be other factors at work, such as "zeitgeist." If, at the same time as a new policy is emerging, there is an ongoing attitudinal shift in society at large toward more egalitarian values, then the impact of female actors is perhaps only marginal.

Gender equality in the everyday lives of citizens: Evidence from the subnational level in Sweden

The link between descriptive and substantive representation is hard to establish. Anne Phillips is extensively cited throughout this book, and she uses the expression "a shot in the dark" with reference to expectations that female politicians will affect politics in specific ways (1995, 83). However, over the last decades, the number of empirical studies in the field has grown and most of them report that female representatives do help to strengthen the position of women in society.[13] One problem here, though, is that the closer one gets to actual outcomes in citizens' everyday lives, the fewer empirical findings there are to report. One important exception is a statistical analysis of child care coverage in Norwegian municipalities in 1975, 1979, 1983, 1987, and 1991, by Kathleen A. Bratton and Leonard P. Ray (2002), who demonstrate that the number of women elected influences policy outputs (increased child care coverage), but the effect of female representatives is not constant, being most obvious in periods of policy innovation. Svaleryd's (2009) study of variation in local public expenditure patterns in Sweden is also worth mentioning, as it supports the finding that an increased number of women elected increases spending on child care.

The tendency to focus on one area at a time merits discussion. Though child care coverage, as noted in the study from Bratton and Ray (2002), is important for women's opportunities to participate in public affairs, this focus could give a one-sided impression of the driving forces of gender equality. A study by Schwindt-Bayer and Mishler (2005), using data from 31 democracies, exemplifies a multidimensional study. The indicators they use are weeks of maternity/parental leave, indices capturing women's political and social equality, and marital equality in law. They conclude that an increase in the number of women elected increases the responsiveness of legislatures to women's policy concerns and enhances perceptions of legitimacy among the electorate, but the authors perceive the effects of having a large number of women elected to be smaller than anticipated in theory.

The debate on how best to measure gender equality in the everyday lives of citizens started in earnest at the UN during the preparation of the *Human Development Reports*. The economists Sudhir Anand and Amartya Sen (1995) developed two indices, the Gender-related Development Index (GDI) and the Gender Empowerment Index (GEM), with the aim of displaying lingering inequalities between women and men. Since then, numerous other indices that measure gender equality have been proposed. Permanyer (2010) reviews several, and exposes theoretical and technical problems with most of them. Taking these experiences into account, the forthcoming analysis at the subnational level in Sweden represents a middle way – including more than one area relevant for gender equality but without collapsing indicators into a single index.

Advantages of studying subnational variation

Sweden and the other Nordic countries are, as stated elsewhere in this book, regularly singled out as among the most women-friendly in the world. As early as the 1980s, the expression "Norden – the passion for equality" had already been coined (Graubard 1986), alluding to values deeply embedded in Nordic society. A more recent study that promotes a cultural approach is that of Inglehart and Norris (2003). Through cross-country comparative research, covering almost all parts of the world, they show that egalitarian values are systematically related to the conditions of women's and men's lives. Inglehart and Norris (ibid.) conclude that modernization underpins cultural change – that is, attitudinal change from traditional to gender-equal values – and that these cultural changes have a major impact on gender-equality processes (see also Liebig 2000; Bergh 2007). With these studies in mind, one of the main advantages of a study on the subnational level is that one can keep cultural factors rather constant.

Another great advantage of studying subnational variation in Sweden is that Swedish municipalities all work within the same legal and institutional framework. Even so, local governments enjoy considerable autonomy from the central government: municipalities set their own budgets and exercise powers of taxation.[14] Previous studies have indicated that there is room for maneuver in the field of gender equality for "ambitious" local governments; strategies that have been used in this regard include integrating a gender perspective into municipal budgeting processes (Pincus 2002) and implementing political decisions to offer full-time employment status to all part-time municipal employees (Lindgren and Vernby 2007).

Equally important for the advancement of this study is the fact that the number of women elected to local councils in Sweden varies considerably. Figure 6.1 shows the proportion of women on municipal councils in Sweden in 1973–2010.[15]

In Sweden elections to the national parliament and to the municipal councils take place at the same time. Thus, the terms are the same at both levels, three years up to the 1994 election, and four years thereafter. Figure 6.1 shows that since 1973 the proportion of women councilors has grown substantially, from an average of 17 percent in the 1973–76 period, to 43 percent in the 2006–10 period. The largest increase occurred between the elections of 1991 and 1994 (a similar increase happened between 1991 and 1994 in the national parliament; see Figure 2.1). However, most noticeable in Figure 6.1 is perhaps the large variation between local councils in Sweden: in the 2006–10 period the proportion of women councilors varied between 58 and 29 percent (a difference of 29 percentage points).

Indicators measuring gender equality in the everyday lives of Swedish citizens

Bratton and Ray's (2002) study of child care coverage in Norwegian municipalities was mentioned previously. Similar results, showing the impact of the number of women elected on child care coverage, were found in a study in Sweden in the early 1980s (Johansson 1983). However, in contemporary Sweden, child care coverage is a less useful indicator of variation in outcomes, since 90 percent of children aged one to six years are registered in day care, and the vast majority are enrolled in municipal day care.

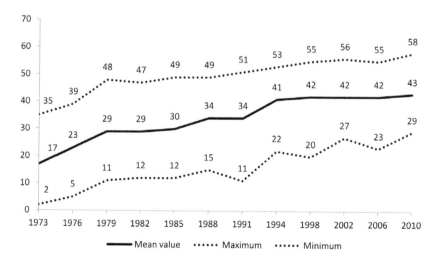

Figure 6.1 Percentage of women on municipal councils in Sweden, 1973–2010 (Statistics Sweden)

The following analysis builds on a study by Wängnerud and Sundell (2012), published in the *European Political Science Review*. The choice of indicators is guided by relevance (they should be significant for the position of women vis-à-vis men), and reliability (there should be trustworthy measures available).[16] The indicators used are percentage employed full time by local government; distribution of parental leave between mothers and fathers (proportion used by fathers); gender gaps in income, unemployment, proportion of low-income earners, and sick days taken per year.

The issue of full-time municipal employment can be seen as a critical test of the link between descriptive and substantive representation of women. Women constitute about 80 percent of municipal employees in Sweden, and data show that the most common reason for women to work part time is that they cannot find suitable full-time work.[17] Previous research has established a link between the *decision* to offer full-time employment to all part-time municipal employees and the presence of women in top executive positions in Swedish municipalities (Lindgren and Vernby 2007). The following analysis is different, since it measures *actual* full-time percentages, but on the basis of previous research this can be considered an "easy" test. If the proportion of women elected has no bearing here, there would be little reason to expect effects in other areas. In a similar vein, the proportion of parental leave used by fathers should perhaps be regarded as an easy test of the theoretical expectations. Although legislation in this area is primarily the task of the national government, local governments are fully capable of implementing various gender equality-positive instruments. For the other indicators it is not equally clear whether they constitute an "easy" or "tough" test of the theoretical expectations.

The role of political parties is a major theme in this book; therefore, party affiliation is included as the most important control variable in the following analysis.[18] However, because prominent scholars like Ronald Inglehart and Pippa Norris (2003) suggest that modernization is the important driving force behind gender-equality processes, a number of socioeconomic indicators are also included in the analysis, the most important being the average municipal population and the average percentage of women and men with tertiary education. The socioeconomic indicators can be seen as proxies for urbanization; previous research in Sweden points out that urban environments generally are more modern and more impregnated with egalitarian values (Forsberg 1997).

Table 6.4 includes results for the three indicators where the percentage of female councilors shows a significant effect: full-time employment for municipal employees, share of parental leave used by fathers, and gender gaps in income. Data for the dependent variables are from the years 2007 or 2008, whereas the independent variables represent averages for the period 1985–2006. For each dependent variable there are two measures: "no level" represents a straightforward women/men ratio, but for "level control" a control for the average level in each municipality is included. For example, in the second analysis municipalities in which women's earnings are greater relative to men's than would be expected from the average income level in the municipality are considered more equal.

The most important result in Table 6.4 is that in municipalities where the number of women elected was comparatively high throughout the 1985–2006 period, parental leave is more equally distributed among mothers and fathers, as more women are employed full time and earn more in relation to men. The theoretical expectation that increasing the proportion of women in elected assemblies will strengthen the position of women vis-à-vis men thus passes the critical test of having an effect on the "easiest" variables – that is, the employment situation for women and parental leave.

Party politics has an effect on two out of three variables in Table 6.4. Women in municipalities where the left-green coalition is stronger than the center-right coalition are, in relation to men, likely to earn more, and they are also more likely to be employed on a full-time basis by the municipality. However, the party variable has no significant effect on the indicator on parental leave.[19]

A further point to note in Table 6.4 is that public sector size (public employees/1,000 capita) has a significant effect on full-time employment in the public sector, and the effect is negative. A reasonable interpretation is that public sector size serves to reduce unemployment among women (Wängnerud and Sundell 2012, 114), but also reduces the proportion of women working full time. Municipalities with larger public sectors tend to employ more women part time than ones with smaller public sectors.

For the other indicators on gender equality in outcomes included in the original study – gender gaps in unemployment, proportion of low-income earners, and sick days taken per year – there is no significant effect on the proportion of female councilors. This leads to several important conclusions: First, the results support the proposition that female representatives will improve conditions for women citizens, though only in some areas. Second, politics in the form of party politics matters as well, with left-green parties having favorable effects for women citizens on a number of indicators.

Another important conclusion from the analysis on the subnational level in Sweden has to do with the widespread use of indices measuring gender equality in the everyday lives of citizens. The choice to use different types of indicators and do separate multivariate regression analyses serves to highlight that there may be different driving forces at work in gender-equality processes: for some dimensions of gender equality, the driving forces at work seem to have more to do with other transformations of society than with the equal distribution of women and men in elected assemblies.

A final theme to discuss before we move on to the analysis at the global level is the microfoundations of the findings from the subnational level in Sweden. The most obvious causal mechanism is that political decisions directly affect behavior. One example, already mentioned, is the possibility of local governments offering full-time employment status to municipal

Table 6.4 The effect of female councilors in Swedish municipalities, 1985–2006, on women's income, full-time employment, and parental leave in relation to men's (OLS regression, unstandardized b-coefficients, standard errors in parentheses)

	Income		Full-time		Parental leave	
	No level	Level control	No level	Level control	No level	Level control
% Female councilors	0.024 (0.066)	0.155** (0.054)	0.785** (0.138)	0.721** (0.134)	-2.859** (0.538)	-2.944** (0.538)
% Left-green parties	0.106** (0.029)	0.064** (0.024)	0.399** (0.061)	0.293** (0.064)	-0.165 (0.240)	-0.162 (0.239)
Female voter turnout, 1921	-0.024 (0.076)	0.036 (0.061)	0.434** (0.159)	0.390* (0.154)	-0.588 (0.623)	-0.677 (0.622)
Public employees/1,000 capita	0.035 (0.020)	0.010 (0.016)	-0.121** (0.041)	-0.083* (0.041)	-0.223 (0.162)	-0.179 (0.163)
Ln (Male education)	-2.299 (1.863)	-1.534 (1.490)	1.779 (3.883)	2.147 (3.748)	7.330 (15.20)	6.786 (15.12)
Ln (Female education)	3.059 (2.560)	8.556** (2.093)	11.76* (5.338)	11.92* (5.151)	-104.1** (20.89)	-96.18** (21.19)
Ln(Population)	-0.821 (0.417)	-1.677** (0.340)	-2.590** (0.870)	-3.593** (0.867)	7.987* (3.405)	6.182 (3.514)
Ln (Area)	1.433** (0.269)	0.836** (0.221)	0.396 (0.562)	0.138 (0.545)	-1.316 (2.198)	-0.709 (2.209)
Average of dependent variable		-0.124** (0.010)		0.478** (0.104)		0.911 (0.470)
Constant	61.31** (4.961)	91.10** (4.627)	24.97* (10.34)	12.93 (10.32)	560.3** (40.48)	497.4** (51.71)

	Income		Full-time		Parental leave	
N	283	283	283	283	283	283
R^2	0.393	0.614	0.510	0.546	0.505	0.511
adj. R^2	0.375	0.601	0.496	0.531	0.490	0.495

(Statistics Sweden and Swedish Social Insurance Agency)

*p < .05 **p < .01. Higher values indicate higher level of gender equality. "No level" means that the dependent variables are ratios (in percentage) of the value for women on the variable compared with the value for men. For example, if the average income for women is SEK200,000 per year, and the average income for men is SEK250,000 per year, the dependent variable is 80 percent. Models designated with "Level control" include a control variable that is the average of the variable for women and men. Full-time employment refers to full-time municipal employment. Table adapted from Wängnerud and Sundell (2012). Data for the dependent variables are from 2007 or 2008. Independent variables represent, in most cases, averages for the period 1985–2006. The number of municipalities in Sweden was 290 in 2008, but the number has varied since that time, and only 283 municipalities for which there were consistent data over time were included in the analysis.

employees. The forerunner in Sweden was the municipality of Bollnäs, which made such a decision in 2001, after which other municipalities followed suit (Lindgren and Vernby 2007). Another prominent example in Swedish politics, also mentioned previously, is that of "Daddy months," which refers to the fact that a substantial part of parental leave can be used only by fathers. As seen in Table 6.3, the first "Daddy month" was introduced in 1995 and another in 2002; after both reforms, the proportion of parental leave used by fathers increased (Erikson 2005). While municipal councils do not have the same regulatory tools as the national parliament in this area, they can initiate projects aimed at leveling out gender differences.

Other processes are obviously connected to more indirect political intervention. In many Swedish municipalities the local government is the biggest employer. Several local-level studies in Sweden support the existence of different priorities among women and men politicians, identifying women, also at this level of government, as the most fervent supporters of gender equality (Hedlund 1996; Gustafsson 2008; Svaleryd 2009; Wängnerud and Högmark 2014). Therefore, it is not far-fetched to believe that women politicians may promote equal hiring practices, equal salaries, and so on, in the public sector. In an in-depth study of three Swedish municipalities, Ingrid Pincus (2002) shows how special local government committees have been established to initiate gender-equality activities in the local authority itself and in the municipality as a whole.

Moreover, having the results in Chapter 2 in mind, in which left-green parties emerged as more gender sensitive than center-right parties, the result that left-green parties have an effect on outcomes in citizens' everyday lives is reasonable. One of the major differences between left-green and center-right parties in Sweden is, as displayed in Chapter 2, the extent to which transformative elements influence ideas on women's representation. Analysis at the local level (Wängnerud and Högmark 2014) shows that councilors affiliated to left-green parties to a higher degree than councilors affiliated to center-right parties support the idea that it is important to have an equal distribution of women and men in elected assemblies, since there will be consequences for policies.

Gender equality in the everyday lives of citizens: Evidence from a worldwide comparison

It is a big step between the subnational level in Sweden and the global arena. The following analysis is, however, important for putting the results for Sweden in perspective. The main thread in this section is the test of driving forces at work in gender-equality processes. Thus, we deal with the same research question as in the other parts of this chapter but with other types of data.

To note in general is the need for theoretical clarity in defining gender equality. Whether a factor such as the proportion of women in elected assemblies increases gender equality in outcomes is contingent on the definition and measurement of gender equality. Equally important to note is that indices including very different dimensions of gender equality may blur the fact that some aspects of gender equality are linked to the presence of female politicians, whereas others are linked to general transformations of society such as modernization processes. Having said that, in cross-country comparative research including a large number of cases, indices may still play an important role. The reasonable solution is to try to use different ways of measuring core concepts and to be careful when drawing conclusions.

Measuring gender equality in the global arena

The UN is a forerunner when it comes to measuring the situation for women worldwide. The UN's measurement of gender equality are, however, most useful in relation to indicators on "general" human development; one idea behind the construction of the GDI was to create a measure of development that penalized countries with greater inequality. As Schüler (2006) shows, however, the GDI is frequently misinterpreted as a direct measure of gender equality, both by academics and by the popular press.

In the forthcoming analysis we shall focus on two straightforward ways of measuring gender equality in the everyday lives of citizens: the Gender Gap Index from the World Economic Forum and the Gender Equity Index from Social Watch. However, some crucial adjustments have been made. The idea is to shed further light on the link between the descriptive and substantive representation of women. The theoretical expectation is that the number of women in elected office is a factor that may cause variations between countries, and therefore it cannot be included in a measurement of the situation – gender equality in everyday life – it is supposed to explain. For the indices to be useful, all aspects concerning women's political participation have had to be deleted from the original indices.[20]

Both indices focus on gender gaps in the economic sector and in education; thus, they are in line with the capability approach brought forward by the UN. The major difference between the indices is that the Gender Gap Index also includes aspects of health and well-being, and in that sense it is more comprehensive than the Gender Equity Index.[21] Table 6.5 includes the highest-ranked countries in the different indices in 2007 and 2012/13.

The results in Table 6.5 show that Sweden is among the top, most gender-equal countries in the world on both occasions. For both indices there is, however, a drop between 2007 and 2012/13. I shall get back to this result in the concluding chapter of this book.

Driving forces behind gender equality in the global arena

Modernization theories have been already discussed. Inglehart and Norris (2003) use the metaphor of the *rising tide* to illustrate what they perceive as

Table 6.5 Top countries in gender-equality rankings from Social Watch and World Economic Forum, 2007 and 2012/13

Gender Equity Index, Social Watch		Gender Gap Index, World Economic Forum	
2007	2012	2007	2013
Sweden	Norway	Sweden	Iceland
Finland	Finland	Norway	Finland
Rwanda	Iceland	Finland	Norway
Norway	Sweden	Iceland	Sweden
Barbados	Denmark	New Zealand	Philippines
Germany	New Zealand	Philippines	Ireland
Denmark	Spain	Germany	New Zealand
Iceland	Mongolia	Denmark	Denmark
Lithuania	Canada	Ireland	Switzerland
Netherlands	Germany	Spain	Nicaragua
Spain	Australia	UK	Belgium

(Social Watch, www.socialwatch.org; and World Economic Forum, www.weforum.org)

the most important driving force in gender-equality processes. They construct a gender-equality scale from measurements of citizens' attitudes toward women as political leaders, women's professional and educational rights, and women's traditional role as mothers. Through extensive cross-country comparative research, covering almost all parts of the world, they show that egalitarian values are systematically related to the conditions of women's and men's lives. In this way they reach the conclusion that modernization underpins cultural change – that is, attitudinal change from traditional to gender-equal values, and that these cultural changes have a major impact on gender equality in citizens' everyday lives.

Inglehart and Norris were not the first to emphasize culture/modernization, and one early argument against this strand of research is that such explanations cannot capture short-term changes (Sainsbury 1993). The cultural perspective has also been criticized for being almost tautological (Rosenbluth et al. 2006). The strand of research focusing on the role of women in parliaments can partly be seen as a response to the aforementioned criticism. To me, what is important is not to determine which perspective can explain the most, but to reach a fine-tuned understanding of the mechanisms at work. Inglehart and Norris present a convincing study; however, this does not mean that modernization is the only factor driving change in gender-equality processes.

In the following analysis the Gender Gap Index and the Gender Equity Index are used as dependent variables. One of the most important explanatory factors is the number of women in national parliaments. The level of democracy and GDP per capita are included as measures of modernization. Two different measures of government capacity – corruption in the public sector and government effectiveness – are also included.[22]

The explanatory factor that merits most discussion is "economic and social rights for women." Data on economic and social rights for women come from the Human Rights Dataset constructed by Cingranelli and Richards (2005). In their measuring of women's rights, Cingranelli and Richards are interested in two things: first, the extensiveness of laws pertaining to women's rights; and second, government practices toward women. The scale ranges from (0), which means that under law there are no rights for women and the government tolerates a high level of discrimination against women, to (3), which means that all or nearly all rights are guaranteed by law, and in practice the government tolerates no or almost no discrimination against women.

It should be noted that Cingranelli and Richards (2005) focus on *formal rights*, such as women's right to enter marriage on a basis of equality with men, the right to participate in social activities, and the right to choose a profession freely without requiring the husband's consent. This makes it different from the dependent variables from the World Economic Forum and Social Watch, which focus on *outcomes*, such as wage equality for similar work, male and female school enrollment, and well-being among men and women. To some extent, Cingranelli and Richards also consider outcomes in that they take into account the implementation of the rights stipulated by law. However, their focus is on legal rights, which are different from the outcome indicators from the indices included. Yoo (2012) uses the same dataset in her study of the impact of domestic and transnational conditions on women's lives, but uses this information to build a dependent variable. Yoo's conclusion after a revision of the data from Cingranelli and Richards is that they "do not measure specific aspects of women's lives, such as fertility rate, secondary education enrollment rate, or incidence of sexual harassment in the workplace" (ibid., 334).

The data from Cingranelli and Richards can be seen as a measure of gender-sensitive legislation. At the same time it can be seen as a measure of group awareness – the extent to which legislators in a specific country are aware of the situation for women citizens (cf. Young 2000).

Table 6.6 includes results from stepwise multivariate regression analyses in which the explanatory factors are introduced one by one. The first dependent variable is the Gender Gap Index, and in this analysis data exist for 115 countries. The second dependent variable is the Gender Equity Index, and in this analysis data exist for 136 countries.[23]

The results in Table 6.6 show that the factor of economic and social rights for women is significant at the 0.01 level in all tests for both of the indices. This is a convincing result, and no other factor displays such a consistent pattern. The introduction of the other explanatory factors contributes to the impression of a robust pattern; results for the measure on economic and social rights for women hold when women in parliament,

Table 6.6 Explanations for variation in gender equality in the everyday lives of citizens, a worldwide comparison (OLS stepwise multivariate regression, coefficients, and adjusted R^2; included)

Explanatory factors	Model 1	Model 2	Model 3	Model 4	Model 5	Model 6
	Gender Gap Index					
Economic and social rights for women	0.048***	0.044***	0.049***	0.050***	0.046***	0.043***
Women in national parliament	–	0.001	0.001	0.001	0.001	0.001
Corruption in public sector	–	–	-0.002	-0.002	0.000	-0.002
Government effectiveness	–	–	–	-0.002	-0.007	-0.013
Level of democracy	–	–	–	–	0.002	0.002
GDP per capita	–	–	–	–	–	0.001
N	115	115	115	115	115	115
Adjusted R^2;	0.366	0.365	.365	0.359	0.360	0.362
	Gender Equity Index					
Economic and social rights for women	9.887***	8.325***	8.294***	7.432**	6.556**	5.875***
Women in national parliament	–	0.201**	0.200**	0.207**	0.214**	0.248***
Corruption in public sector	–	–	0.014	-1.373*	-1.164	-1.515**
Government effectiveness	–	–	–	3.737**	2.820	1.338
Level of democracy	–	–	–	–	0.469	0.594
GDP per capita	–	–	–	–	–	0.258
N	136	136	136	136	136	136
Adjusted R^2;	0.379	0.396	0.391	0.408	0.413	0.419

Independent variables: (3) Economic and social rights for women – varies between 0 (no economic/social rights for women under law) and 3 (all or nearly all of women's economic/social rights are guaranteed by law). Index constructed on Cingranelli and Richards (2005). (4) Women in national parliament – percentage of women in single or lower house (interparliamentary union). (5) Corruption in the public sector – Transparency International data, ranges between 10 (highly clean) and 0 (highly corrupt). (6) Government effectiveness – World Bank data, normalized with a mean of 0 and a standard deviation of 1 (implying that virtually all scores lie between -2.5 and 2.5). (7) Democracy – average index built on Freedom House and Polity data, scale ranges from 0 (least democratic) to 10 (most democratic). (8) GDP per capita – real GDP per capita in thousands of US dollars.

corruption, government effectiveness, level of democracy, and GDP per capita are introduced. It is also worth noting that the factor of women in national parliament is not significant in the analysis where the Gender Gap Index serves as dependent variable; however, it is significant in the analysis where the Gender Equity Index serves as a dependent variable (even when controlling for the other explanatory factors).

One thing that could cause the factor of women in parliament to show significant results for the Gender Equity Index but not for the Gender Gap Index is that the number of cases included in each set of regressions varies, and therefore regressions for the Gender Equity Index were done in a smaller sample that included only those countries with values also on the Gender Gap Index (a subset of 113 countries). The factor of women in parliament remained significant in these tests, which means that sample selection is not the explanation for the deviant result. The explanation may concern the underlying variables included in each of the indices. The Gender Gap Index, but not the Gender Equity Index, includes health aspects along with aspects of education and economic activity. The results in Table 6.6 are thus concrete illustrations of the point made previously; scholars need to be careful when choosing indicators of outcomes in the everyday lives of citizens. Also, in the analysis at the subnational level in Sweden (Wängnerud and Sundell 2012), indicators related to health displayed a null result when correlated with the number of women elected. Once again, some aspects of gender equality may have more to do with slow transformations of society than with more rapid changes such as the increased number of women in decision-making positions.

The results presented in this section do not rule out the possibility that the number of women elected to office is important for the level of gender equality in society. The design applied is not ideal for capturing effects of such transformations. However, it is interesting to note that the effect of the factor of economic and social rights for women shows such a strong and robust pattern. One way to interpret this result is to say that gender-sensitive legislation matters and that future research needs to pay more attention to "feminism" and "group awareness" than to the sheer number of women elected. Another way to interpret the results, however, is that laws pertaining to women's rights are a mechanism through which the presence of women in parliament affects gender equality in outcomes. The causal chain would then look something like (i) female legislators press for gender-sensitive legislation, and (ii) find allies among men legislators, to (iii) create gender-sensitive legislation, which (iv) when implemented forcefully affects the position of women vis-à-vis men in society at large.

The role that parliaments play in transformations of society

It is quite clear that parliaments play a role in transformations of society. My aim is not to say that x percent can be attributed to the Riksdag and x

percent to modernization processes or political actors other than elected representatives. One important observation that comes out of this chapter is that in Sweden the bulk of gender-equality policies have targeted women. It is mainly from the mid-1980s and onwards that we find gender-equality policies targeting men. This can perhaps be attributed to the fact that women, since the 1985 election, constitute a critical mass in the Riksdag. The interpretation is then that a critical mass is crucial for the emergence of a multifaceted way of understanding a policy area such as gender equality.

One of the major changes in Swedish society since the 1960s is the increased participation of women in the labor force. The Labor Force Surveys show that in 1970 60 percent of women aged 20–64 years in Sweden were in the labor force; in 2011 the corresponding figure was 82.5 percent (plus another 6.4 percent who were unemployed). The largest increase is among women working long hours part time – that is, 20–34 hours per week. Among men, figures remain stable during the same time period: in 2011 88.7 percent of men aged 20–64 years in Sweden were in the labor force (plus another 6.7 percent considered unemployed). This can be contrasted to changes taking place in parental leave. The statistics tell us that in 1974, when men got the right to parental leave on the same terms as women, no days for which parental allowance was paid were claimed by men; in 2011 the corresponding figure was 24 percent. Thus, men in Sweden are becoming integrated into traditionally female spheres, but progress is relatively slow. The interpretation I make is that gender-equality policies targeting men are a contested area in Swedish politics, and therefore, far-reaching changes are harder to achieve than in other areas (cf. Waylen 2007).

A final theme to discuss is the gender-neutral language used in official Swedish documents on gender equality. Mieke Verloo (2005) points to the ambivalence inherent in gender mainstreaming strategies. Verloo concludes that a well-functioning strategy needs to be "conceptualized as a process of changing processes and as ongoing (feminist) political struggles" (ibid., 361). There is an obvious risk of goal formulations being mistaken for descriptions of reality, and to be *gender sensitive* in the deep sense, official policies should articulate the wished-for changes in more specific ways. In Sweden, women are not in a disadvantaged position vis-à-vis men in all dimensions of life, and there is need for gender-equality policies targeting men as well as those targeting women. The point I want to make is that in order to be successful, policies and strategies need to be very consciously composed.

Notes

1 Swedish Parliamentary Surveys 1994 and 2006.
2 In this chapter the report from Statistics Sweden, *Women and Men in Sweden: Facts and Figures*, plays an important role. Statistics Sweden is a government agency, and the statistics produced are used as a basis for decision making, debates, and research. Statistics Sweden also has a coordinating role for the official statistics of Sweden (www.scb.se).

3 These organizations have been chosen as having a good international reputation, and their indices are often referred to. Social Watch describes itself as an "international NGO [nongovernmental organization] watchdog network monitoring poverty eradication and gender equality" (www.socialwatch.org). The World Economic Forum is "an independent international organization committed to improving the state of the world by engaging leaders in partnerships to shape global, regional and industry agendas" (www.weforum.org).
4 United Nations *Global Human Development Report 2006*.
5 Martha Nussbaum collaborated with Amartya Sen at the World Institute for Development Economics Research in the 1980s. In her book (Nussbaum 2000) she describes the main differences between their perspectives.
6 The UN included commitments to gender mainstreaming in the Beijing Declaration and Platform for Action. Additional commitments comprise those in the outcome of the 23rd special session of the General Assembly, the Millennium Declaration, and a variety of resolutions and decisions of the UN General Assembly, the Security Council, the Economic and Social Council, and the Commission on the Status of Women (www.unwomen.org).
7 The latest time-use study in Sweden (2010/11) shows that during a typical week women spend an average of 26 hours on unpaid work, while men spend about 21 hours. In 1990/91 women spent an average of 33 hours on unpaid work per week, while the corresponding figure for men was 21 hours. Thus, the gender gap has decreased but this is a result of women doing less unpaid work. The amount of time spent on unpaid work varies considerably, not only between women and men, but also through the different stages of the life cycle (*Women and Men in Sweden: Facts and Figures*, 2012, 39).
8 This description refers to organization during the 2010/14 term.
9 I would like to thank Bo Rothstein for pointing this out.
10 Included in the forthcoming analyses are laws/regulations presented as important for progress in the area of gender equality by Statistics Sweden in their report *Women and Men in Sweden: Facts and Figures*, 2012, 7–12. Some regulations are not legislation that has passed the Riksdag, but agreements between, for example, employers and unions. Important to note is that one type of governing coalition may have initiated a new policy that was made into law under another regime. A case in point is the "Daddy month," made into law in 1995 under a Social Democratic regime, but initiated by the center-right coalition in cabinet during the 1991/94 term.
11 Parental allowance in Sweden is explained in detail in *Women and Men in Sweden: Facts and Figures*, 2012, 44–46.
12 In 2014 a proposal on a third nontransferable month was being negotiated among key actors in the Riksdag.
13 Some of the most important studies are: Diaz 2005; Dodson 2006; Lovenduski 2005; Reingold 2000; Schwindt-Bayer 2010; Skjeie 1992; Swers 2013; Thomas 1994; and Wängnerud 2000.
14 Svaleryd (2009, 190) reports that Swedish municipal spending constitutes more than 40 percent of Swedish public spending. Most municipal spending concerns care for the elderly, education, and child care.
15 Currently, the number of municipalities in Sweden is 290. The number of municipal councilors varies from 31 (municipalities with fewer than 12,000 inhabitants) to 101 (Stockholm, the capital).
16 Therefore, for example, an area such as violence against women is excluded.
17 This is found in the Labor Force Survey 2011 (see *Women and Men in Sweden: Facts and Figures*, 2012, 56). The second most common reason for women to work part time is care of children.

18 The variable distinguishes between average proportions of seats for left-green parties versus center-right parties, 1985–2006 (see Chapter 2 of this book for categorization of parties).
19 Party politics had an effect on four out of six variables in the original study: women in municipalities where the left-green coalition was stronger than the center-right coalition were, in relation to men, likely to earn more, and less likely to be unemployed or be among the low-income earners; they were also more likely to be employed on a full-time basis by the municipality (Wängnerud and Sundell 2012, 114).
20 I am grateful to Marcus Samanni, who conducted the empirical analysis in this section and also gave helpful comments on design and the interpretation of results.
21 The composition variables included from the Social Watch index are primary school enrollment, secondary school enrollment, tertiary education enrollment, adult literacy rate, labor force gap, non-vulnerable employment, and estimated income gap. The variables included from the World Economic Forum index are female labor force participation over male value, wage equality between women and men for similar work (converted to female-over-male ratio), female estimated earned income over male value, female professional and technical workers over male value, female literacy rate over male value, female net primary enrollment rate over male value, female net secondary enrollment rate over male value, female gross tertiary enrollment ratio over male value, sex ratio at birth (converted to female-over-male ratio), and female healthy life expectancy over male value.
22 The dataset used is the Quality of Government Dataset available from the Quality of Government Institute at the University of Gothenburg, www.qog.pol.gu.se (Teorell et al. 2009).
23 The countries included in the different samples are from all parts of the world, with somewhat better coverage given to the countries in Europe and America than elsewhere.

Bibliography

Anand, Sudhir and Amartya Sen. 1995. *Gender Inequality in Human Development: Theories and Measurement*. Occasional Paper no. 19.. New York: United Nations Development Program, Human Development Report Office.

Bergh, Johannes. 2007. "Gender Attitudes and Modernization Processes." *International Journal of Public Opinion Research* 19(1): 5–23.

Bergqvist, Christina *et al.* 2000. *Equal Democracies? Gender and Politics in the Nordic Countries*. Oslo: Norwegian University Press.

Bratton, Kathleen A. and Leonard P. Ray. 2002. "Descriptive Representation, Policy Outcomes, and Municipal Day-care Coverage in Norway." *American Journal of Political Science* 46(2): 428–437.

Cedstrand, Sofie. 2011. *Från idé till politisk verklighet. Föräldrapolitiken i Sverige och Danmark*. Umeå: Boréa.

Childs, Sarah and Mona Lena Krook. 2006. "Should Feminists Give Up on a Critical Mass? A Contingent Yes." *Politics & Gender* 2(4): 522–530.

Cingranelli, David L. and David L. Richards. 2005. "Human Rights Dataset, Version 2005.10.12." www.humanrightsdata.org.

Dahlerup, Drude. 1988. "From a Small to a Large Minority: Women in Scandinavian Politics." *Scandinavian Political Studies* 4: 275–298.

Dahlerup, Drude. 2006. "The Story of the Critical Mass." *Politics & Gender* 2(4): 511–522.

Diaz, Mercedes M. 2005. *Representing Women? Female Legislators in West European Parliaments.* Colchester: ECPR Press.
Dodson, Deborah L. 2006. *The Impact of Women in Congress.* Oxford: Oxford University Press.
Erikson, Josefina. 2011. *Strider om mening. En dynamisk frameanalys av den svenska sexköpslagen.* Uppsala: Uppsala University. Skrifter utgivna av Statsvetenskapliga föreningen i Uppsala, 180.
Forsberg, Gunnel. 1997. "Rulltrapperegioner och social infrastruktur." In *Om makt och kön – in spåren av offentliga organisationers omvandling* (SOU 1997:83), ed. Elisabeth Sundin. Stockholm: SOU.
Freidenvall, Lenita. 2006. *Vägen till Varannan Damernas. Om kvinnorepresentation, kvotering och kandidaturval i svensk politik 1970–2002.* Stockholm: Stockholm University.
Graubard, Stephen R., ed. 1986. *Norden – The Passion for Equality.* Oslo: Norwegian University Press.
Gustafsson, Anette. 2008. *Könsmakt och könsbaserade intressen: Om könspolitisk representation i svensk kommunalpolitik.* Gothenburg: University of Gothenburg.
Hedlund, Gun. 1996. *Det handlar om prioriteringar: Kvinnors villkor och intressen i lokal politik.* Örebro: Örebro Studies in Politics.
Hirdman, Yvonne. 2014. *Vad bör göras? Jämställdhet och politik under femtio år.* Stockholm: Ordfront.
Högmark, Anna and Lena Wängnerud. 2014. "Den politiska betydelsen av kön." In *Svenska politiker*, ed. David Karlsson and Mikael Gilljam. Stockholm: Santérus Förlag.
Inglehart, Ronald and Pippa Norris. 2003. *Rising Tide: Gender Equality and Cultural Change Around the World.* Cambridge: Cambridge University Press.
Jakobsson, Niklas and Andreas Kotsadam. 2013. "The Law and Economics of International Sex Slavery: Prostitution Laws and Trafficking for Sexual Exploitation." *European Journal of Law and Economics* 35: 87–107.
Johansson, Leif (1983) "Kommunal servicevariation." In *De nya kommunerna. En sammanfattning av den kommunaldemokratiska forskningsgruppens undersökningar*, ed. Lars Strömberg and Jörgen Westerståhl. Stockholm: Liber Förlag.
Karlsson, Gunnel. 1996. *Från broderskap till systerskap. Det socialdemokratiska kvinnoförbundets kamp för inflytande och makt i SAP.* Lund: Arkiv.
Liebig, Brigitte. 2000. "Perspectives on Gender Cultures in Elites." In *Gendering Elites: Economic and Political Leadership in 27 Industrialized Societies*, ed. Mina Vianello and Gwen Moore. London: MacMillan, 220–232.
Lindgren, Karl-Oskar and Kåre Vernby. 2007. "Om kvinnorepresentation och rätten till heltid." *Kommunal Ekonomi och Politik* 11(4): 7–31.
Lindvert, Jessica. 2002. *Feminism som politik. Sverige och Australien 1960–1990.* Umeå: Boréa.
Lovenduski, Joni. 2005. *Feminizing Politics.* Cambridge: Polity Press.
Nussbaum, Martha C. 2000. *Women and Human Development: The Capabilities Approach.* Cambridge: Cambridge University Press.
Permanyer, Iñaki. 2010. "The Measurement of Multidimensional Gender Inequality: Continuing the Debate." *Social Indicators Research* 95: 181–198.
Phillips, Anne. 1995. *The Politics of Presence.* Oxford: Oxford University Press.
Pincus, Ingrid. 2002. *The Politics of Gender Equality Policy: A Study of Implementation and Non-Implementation in Three Swedish Municipalities.* Örebro: Örebro Studies in Political Science.

Reingold, Beth. 2000. *Representing Women: Sex, Gender, and Legislative Behavior in Arizona and California*. Chapel Hill: University of North Carolina Press.
Rönnbäck, Josefin. 2004*Politikens genusgränser. Den kvinnliga rösträttsrörelsen och kampen för kvinnors politiska medborgarskap 1902–1921*. Stockholm: Atlas akademi.
Rosenbluth, Frances, Rob Salmond and Michael F. Thies. 2006. "Welfare Works: Explaining Female Legislative Representation." *Politics & Gender* 2: 165–192.
Sainsbury, Diane. 1993 "The Politics of Increased Women's Representation: The Swedish Case." In *Gender and Party Politics*, ed. Joni Lovenduski and Pippa Norris. London: Sage.
Schüler, Dana. 2006. "The Uses and Misuses of the Gender-related Development Index and Gender Empowerment Measure: A Review of the Literature." *Journal of Human Development* 7(2): 161–181.
Schwindt-Bayer, Leslie A.. 2010. *Political Power and Women's Representation in Latin America*. Oxford: Oxford University Press.
Schwindt-Bayer, Leslie A. and William Mishler. 2005. "An Integrated Model of Women's Representation." *Journal of Politics* 67(2): 407–428.
Skjeie, Hege. 1992. *Den politiske betydningen av kjønn. En studie av norsk topp-politikk*. Rapport 92:11. Oslo: Institutt Samfunnsforskning.
Svaleryd, Helena. 2009. "Women's Representation and Public Spending." *European Journal of Political Economy* 25: 186–198.
Swers, Michele L.. 2013. *Women in the Club: Gender and Policy Making in the Senate*. Chicago: University of Chicago Press.
Teorell, Jan et al. 2009. "The Quality of Government Dataset," version June 17, 2009. Gothenburg: University of Gothenburg, The Quality of Government Institute. www.qog.pol.gu.se.
Thomas, Susan. 1994. *How Women Legislate*. Oxford: Oxford University Press.
Verloo, Mieke. 2005. "Displacement and Empowerment: Reflections on the Concept and Practice of the Council of Europe Approach to Gender Mainstreaming and Gender Equality." *Social Politics* 12(3): 344–365.
Wängnerud, Lena. 2000. "Testing the Politics of Presence: Women's Representation in the Swedish Riksdag." *Scandinavian Political Studies* 23(1): 67–91.
Wängnerud, Lena and Anna Högmark (2014) "Den politiska betydelsen av kön." In *Svenska politiker. Om de folkvalda i riksdag, landsting och kommuner*, ed. David Karlsson and Mikael Gilljam. Stockholm: Santérus förlag.
Wängnerud, Lena and Anders Sundell. 2012. "Do Politics Matter? Women in Swedish Local Elected Assemblies 1970–2010 and Gender Equality in Outcomes." *European Political Science Review* 4(1): 97–120.
Waylen, Georgina. 2007. *Engendering Transitions: Women's Mobilization, Institutions, and Gender Outcomes*. Oxford: Oxford University Press.
Yoo, Eunhye. 2012. "The Impact of Domestic and Transnational Conditions." *Politics & Gender* 8: 304–340.
Young, Iris M. 2000. *Inclusion and Democracy*. Oxford: Oxford University Press.

7 The politics of feminist awareness

The results in this book can be presented as a double projection: increases in the number of women elected propel gender-equality processes, but the higher the number gets, the less important in transformations toward a women-friendly society is the number of women elected. This has to do with changes in the party system, most notably ideological shifts, but also with changes in attitudes of elected representatives, most notably the increased importance of group awareness. In this concluding chapter I shall present a revised version of the gender-sensitive parliament and develop the reasoning on the most important findings.

Ideological shifts with a bearing on gender-equality processes

If we start with ideological shifts, it is quite apparent that processes related to gender equality need to be analyzed against the backdrop of a wider political landscape. In Sweden one of the most notable changes taking place since the 1970s has been the rise of the Conservative Party as the major player among the center-right parties. We have seen (Figure 2.2) how the Conservative Party, over time, has moved slightly toward the middle of the ideological left–right scale. Even clearer, however, is how the Liberal Party and the Center Party have moved toward the right. This means that the gap between the Conservative Party and the other center-right parties has decreased significantly. The effect of this shift is the emergence of two rather distinct blocs in the party system – the demarcation having to do not only with left–right ideology but also with gender-equality norms.

However, it is not as simple as being able to say that left–right ideology and gender-equality norms always go hand in hand as two symbiotic phenomena. In the 1990s the Liberal Party and the Center Party were quite strongly impregnated with feminist ideas of reversal, which are ideas that aim at transformations of current politics. However, over time ideas of reversal have lost ground and the center-right parties have, as a group/bloc, come to be dominated by feminist ideas of inclusion which aim at the inclusion of women in the world "as it is" (Squires 1999; Verloo 2005).

The point I want to make is that developments could have been different. I believe that research on women in parliaments can make more use of exposure-based approaches (Bolzendahl and Myers 2004) in their understandings of dynamics within and between political parties. The push toward convergence among center-right parties started in the early 2000s when the four center-right parties formed "the Alliance." The Alliance meant close collaboration and all sorts of encounters between elected representatives of these parties. The interpretation I make is that representatives of the Conservative Party thus became more strongly exposed to feminist ideals than they otherwise would have been, but at the same time, since they were the leading party within the Alliance coalition, Conservative representatives could influence the content of these ideals. Key here is that the Liberal Party and the Center Party in the past decade have been operating in the shadow of the Conservative Party. We can observe how a mix of ideas of reversal and inclusion ends up in a dominance of ideas of inclusion (Figure 2.4). In 2010 it is only the left-green parties that differ from the Conservative Party in their support for ideas of reversal (Table 2.2).

The lesson to be learned is that the "gender-sensitive party" is not a one-dimensional phenomenon. Research focusing on the role of political parties in processes related to gender equality should strive for measures that capture norms pertaining to expectations of transformation. As previously stated, changes do not just happen, and if women politicians are acting in a milieu where ideas of reversal are reasonably well established, that may boost endeavors to bring forth women's interests and concerns.

Most indicators in this book point in the direction of the ideological left–right dimension increasing in importance between 1985 and 2010, but that is not only because left-leaning parties are "leftist" and thus, in general, more impregnated with egalitarian values. I would say that the important factor is that left-green parties embrace a mix of feminist ideas of inclusion and reversal. Counterfactual reasoning is always problematic, but the mix of ideas of inclusion and reversal might have looked different within the center-right bloc if the Liberal Party and the Center Party had been stronger when the Alliance coalition was formed.

The role of group awareness

Elected representatives' approaches to different groups in society can be seen as part of ideological reasoning. From previous research in Sweden and the other Nordic countries we know that MPs from leftist parties tend to place strong emphasis on the representation of different social groups such as women, immigrants, and wage earners/laborers. MPs from right-wing parties are relatively less inclined to emphasize such groups and relatively more inclined to view business interests as important to promote in parliamentary work (Esaiasson 2000).

The result for the approach of Swedish MPs toward women as a group is striking in how it changes over time. In the 1980s this is clearly a gendered topic: women MPs are strongly committed to the task of representing women's interests and concerns. In the 1994 election, when the feminist network, the Support Stockings, put pressure on the established political parties regarding feminism and gender equality, commitment to women as a group becomes strong in most party groups, and especially strong among newcomers in the Riksdag. In 2010 the commitment to women's interests and concerns is particularly strong among women MPs, and also MPs from the Left Party and the Social Democratic Party (Table 3.2).

An important lesson to be learned is that one cannot take it for granted that more women in parliament means increased awareness of women as a group. Nor can one take for granted that external shocks such as the activities of the feminist network, the Support Stockings, will leave, once and for all, their mark on attitudes and behaviors of MPs. The analyses in this book show that the proportion of MPs who are strongly committed to representing women's interests and concerns remains, overall, remarkably stable between 1985 and 2010 (during this period the proportion of women in the Swedish parliament increases from 32 to 45 percent). However, *who* these committed MPs are varies across time. Even more important to point out is that the effect of being a committed MP varies across time. At the end of the period studied group awareness has a visible effect on a number of indicators used to measure support for women's interests and concerns: priorities for areas such as gender-equality policy and welfare politics, attitudes toward proposals such as banning all forms of pornography and introducing a six-hour workday, and willingness to contact cabinet ministers on behalf of women/women's organizations.

The principles of gender-sensitive parliaments: a revised model

Based on the analyses presented in this book I suggest that the two-dimensional model previously presented (Figure 1.1), which distinguishes between the numbers of women elected and gender sensitivity, should be made three-dimensional and should also include group awareness as a driving force behind a gender-sensitive parliament. The theory on group awareness cannot replace the theory on the politics of presence in studies of women, gender, and politics. They both need to be taken into account. What the results in this book show, however, is how over time they become more and more distinct phenomena. Figure 7.1 illustrates how group awareness between 1985 and 2010 becomes, in itself, a driving force toward a gender-sensitive parliament.

In Figure 7.1 I use the term "feminist awareness" instead of "group awareness." This signals that we need to find ways to distinguish between different approaches to women as a group. Feminist ideas can come in many forms, and *strength* in commitment seems to matter, but so does the *type* of commitment. The indicators used in this book can certainly be refined, but the results demonstrate that it is worth the effort to measure "feminist awareness" as a multidimensional concept. The results also demonstrate that it is worth the effort to investigate feminist awareness both at the level of individual MPs and at the level of political parties.

Is the Riksdag a gender-sensitive parliament?

Sweden is losing ground in rankings such as those produced by the World Economic Forum (the Gender Gap Index) and Social Watch (the Gender Equity Index). Are these results worthy of attention? Sweden is one of the most gender-equal countries in the world – does it really matter whether it is the *most* gender-equal country or not? From a global perspective worrying about the drop from number one to number four in the rankings mentioned above is like raising a tempest in a teapot. However, if one adds these results to other findings in this book, I believe that they point to the fact that there is no linear process leading to gender equality.

In Figure 7.2 I situate the contemporary Swedish Riksdag in the tension between a high number of women elected and a gender-sensitive parliament. There is no exact way to calculate the placement of the three dimensions included, but in subsequent sections I shall explain my reasoning. The arrows in Figure 7.2 symbolize that I assess a positive trend when it comes to the situation for women in terms of internal parliamentary working

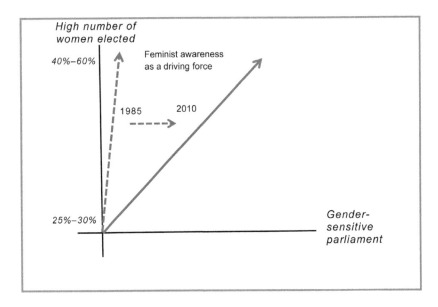

Figure 7.1 Feminist awareness as a driving force toward a gender-sensitive parliament

procedures, but when it comes to the room for women's interests and concerns, and for the production of gender-sensitive legislation, I assess that progress on these is currently at more of a standstill. The placement on the horizontal axis also matters: the working procedures are closer to the ideal of a gender-sensitive parliament than the other two dimensions (which does not mean that everything is perfect, just relatively better).

Internal parliamentary working procedures

At the beginning of the 1980s Elina Haavio-Mannila and colleagues made a distinction between hierarchical and functional gender structures in their study on women in Nordic politics (Haavio-Mannila et al. 1983). Since then, functional gender structures – sometimes referred to as horizontal sex segregation – have received a great deal of attention. The analyses in this book show how certain structures related to political content emerge in the standing committees in the Swedish parliament in the 1980s. After the 1994 election there is a sharp decline, and even though patterns of "femininity" and "masculinity" are not totally gone, they are much weaker today than they used to be. Scholars like Drude Dahlerup and Monique Leyenaar (2013) and Catherine Bolzendahl (2014) see this change as an important indicator in the development of a gender-egalitarian institution.

The conclusion I reach after examining the pattern in the standing committees together with results from other indicators on internal parliamentary

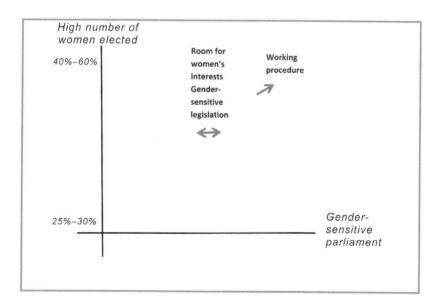

Figure 7.2 Situating the contemporary Swedish Riksdag in the tension between a high number of women elected and gender sensitivity

136   *The politics of feminist awareness*

working procedures, such as MPs' assessments of the working conditions in their own party groups and the ability to impact their own party groups' positions, is that scholars are running the risk of overestimating the importance of a balanced/gender-neutral assignment of committee positions. Hierarchical gender structures are, however, of the utmost importance to study. We have seen that being in a power position in the parliament significantly affects an MP's ability to impact his or her own party group (Table 4.6).

One reason for stating that there is a risk of overemphasizing the importance of balanced/gender-neutral committee assignments is that the increased gender neutrality in Swedish standing committees has not been followed by a reduced gender gap when it comes to MPs' assessments of their working conditions. Women were more critical than men in the 1980s, when there was a stark gender structure in committee assignments, but they were also more critical than men in 2010, when the gender structure was much less apparent. Gender gaps are particularly persistent in the assessment of working conditions in the party groups (Table 4.3), and qualitative interviews reveal dissatisfaction with attitudes and norms linked to what is regarded as a "good" politician. More women than men oppose the norm of being a loyal party worker in the sense of always being available for the party (Ahlbäck Öberg et al. 2007).

Taking half a step back, I still perceive the decline in gender structures in the Swedish standing committees as important, because this is a visible sign of commitment to gender equality by the parties' leaderships. In 1994 when the feminist network the Support Stockings was active, all established political parties in Sweden made promises to ensure visible change. The decline in the gender structures in the standing committees shows that this applied not only to the external party lists but also to internal bodies of power in the Riksdag. The MPs who entered the Riksdag in the 1994 election were no different from MPs in previous years when it comes to preferences for committees – more women than men preferred a seat on a committee in the area of social welfare and, conversely, more men than women preferred a seat on a committee in the area of economy/technology – but party leaderships made an effort to break with previous patterns of femininity and masculinity. More detailed analysis shows that this break was visible in most parties in the Riksdag (Wängnerud 1998, 62–63).

Thus, taken together I perceive a positive trend when it comes to internal parliamentary working procedures, and even though women still meet certain obstacles, these obstacles are not so severe that they prevent women in the Riksdag from having power and influence.

Room for women's interests and concerns

The analyses in this book related to the room for women's interests and concerns show a rather mixed result. On the one hand, over time we see more male MPs displaying a personal interest in the area of welfare politics, and party affiliation decreasing in importance (Table 5.3). This means that MPs' interest in this area, which is central to the everyday lives of women citizens, becomes more evenly distributed. It is reasonable to conclude that there has been a shift of emphasis as the number of women in the parliament has increased, with certain kinds of welfare politics being accorded greater scope and a more prominent place on the political agenda (cf. Bergqvist et al. 2000; Skjeie 1992, Wängnerud 2000).

On the other hand, we have seen that the area of gender equality – this refers to topics such as quotas, gender discrimination, and women's rights more broadly – is not, in a similar manner, accorded greater scope in the Riksdag. During the whole period studied, about 10–15 percent of MPs express a personal interest in this area, and almost all of these MPs are women (Figure 5.1). In addition, there is, over time, a decline in MPs' personal contact with women's organizations (Table 5.1), and the indicators on attitudes toward a number of concrete policy proposals show that women MPs are increasingly "at odds" with women voters. For example, women voters strongly support the proposals to ban all forms of pornography and to introduce a six-hour workday, and in the 1980s the support for these proposals was also strong among female MPs. The attitudes among female voters remain rather stable, but in the 2000s the support for these proposals has decreased significantly among female MPs.

The definition of women's interests used in this book is centered on the concept of self-determination. At heart is the idea that people – women as well as men – need a sufficient income, education, good health, and political freedom to realize their potential as human beings. Self-determination is about having real choices (Phillips 2007, 101). Along this line of reasoning it was stated that in gender-equal democracies, women and men are able to choose between political alternatives that address their specific concerns. A bottom line was set: A politics dominated by economy, taxes, and jobs does not reflect women's interests and concerns, since it will not provide women with a sufficient basis for making significant and meaningful choices.

The starting point for the analysis is thus a theoretical definition of women's interests that emphasizes choice and politicization rather than a specific content. From that point of view it is reasonable to conclude that there is room for women's interests and concerns on the political agenda, and moreover, that the room has become more generous over time. However, what I suggest in Figure 7.2 is a standstill, and the main reason for this assessment is that there are clear signs of elected representatives becoming more and more at odds with women voters on attitudes toward a number of concrete policy proposals. Since citizens/voters are the funding actors in democratic states, this is a serious matter.

I believe that there is a need for thorough revisions of the concept of women's interests. From my point of view, self-determination is a good starting point, and at one level of abstraction the three-part definition suggested is useful – that is, the recognition of women as a social category, the acknowledgement of the unequal balance of power between the sexes, and the occurrence of policies designed to increase self-determination of female citizens. Problems arise in the next step, in the contextualization of these interests. In this book, "the Scandinavian welfare state" is used as background for the analysis, but future work could focus on more narrowly defined contexts and, for example, take class aspects into account. Arguably, that would lead to a greater focus on questions of content. Important to bear in mind is that definitions of interests cannot be too esoteric. Hanna Pitkin (1967, 156) reminds us that recognizing interests is a matter of concretizing that which various groups can expect to gain through political inclusion.

"Intersectionality" has long been a buzzword in feminist studies, and I agree that class, ethnicity, age, sexuality, and so on are important factors. There are always tradeoffs in research, and the analyses in this book cover a rather long period of time and several different aspects of the parliamentary process. The focus on the women/men dichotomy is based on the desire to make an in-depth study. What comes out as an important side result in this book, however, is a visualization of the fluidity of the sex/gender category – indeed, the effect of sex/gender is not the same in the 1980s as in the 2000s.

The production of gender-sensitive legislation

My overall assessment also for the dimension of the production of gender-sensitive legislation is that there is a standstill in the development toward a gender-sensitive parliament. The analyses regarding this dimension are more "impressionistic" than other analyses presented in this book. To some extent this characterization builds on the fact that I have relied on officially sanctioned lists of what is to be regarded as gender-sensitive legislation instead of independently collected data. The official documents have, however, been supplemented with two sets of analyses on the link between descriptive and substantive representation of women: one focusing on outcomes in the everyday life of Swedish citizens and the other focusing on the situation for women vis-à-vis men from a global perspective.

One of the most significant results coming out of these analyses is that the proportion of women in elected assemblies is important for some dimensions of citizens' everyday lives, but not for others. In the case of Sweden the number of women elected to local councils had an effect on the percentage of employees (most of whom are women) employed full time by local government, the distribution of parental leave between mothers and fathers (the proportion used by fathers), and gender gaps in income. However, the number of women elected to local councils did not have an effect on gender gaps in unemployment, proportion of low-income earners, or sick days taken per year.

In the analysis of the global arena, covering more than 100 countries, the proportion of women in national parliaments was significantly related to the Gender Equity Index, produced by Social Watch, but not to the Gender Gap Index, produced by the World Economic Forum. Both indices focus on gender gaps in the economic sector and in education. The major difference between the indices is that the Gender Gap Index also includes aspects of health and well-being, and in that sense it is more comprehensive than the Gender Equity Index. What we can learn from these studies on the subnational level and in the global arena is that we need to study processes related to gender equality from a long-term as well as a short-term perspective. For some areas of gender equality it is reasonable to believe that the composition of parliaments – more specifically, the proportion of women elected – has a significant effect. For other areas the role that parliaments play is more remote, and the driving forces at work may be modernization (Inglehart and Norris 2003) or women's non-parliamentary organizations (Htun and Weldon 2012; Yoo 2012).

Taking a bird's-eye view of the production of gender-sensitive legislation in Sweden, one can see an interesting sequencing of strategies: when formal rights for women have been secured, legislation targeting women as workers becomes more frequent, and then at the end of the period studied, legislation targeting men as caregivers becomes more frequent. Another interesting result in these analyses is that the language used in the official rhetoric is rather gender neutral. The overall objective for gender-equality policy in Sweden is to ensure that women and men have equal power to shape society and their own lives, but there are few hints as to what this means in terms of changed behavior among women and changed behavior among men (Table 6.1). Mieke Verloo (2005) points to the ambivalence inherent in gender mainstreaming strategies, the kind of strategies on which Swedish gender-equality policy is modeled. Verloo (ibid., 361) concludes that a well-functioning strategy needs to recognize ongoing struggles, and the lack of such recognition in official documents may be part of the explanation for why developments toward gender equality in the everyday lives of citizens do not happen faster.

How far will these results be able to travel?

Sweden has been presented as a useful laboratory in which to study the complicated relationship between descriptive and substantive representation of women. I would say that the most important result is that research needs to find ways of including measures on group awareness/feminist awareness in studies on parliamentary processes. The ways that elected representatives approach social groups are important for key indicators such as priorities, attitudes, and policy promotion. The question arises: How generally valid is this result? The question can be split in two: first, is the result valid for categories other than gender, and second, is it valid for countries other than Sweden?

A comparison of gender, class, and ethnicity

The Swedish Parliamentary Surveys allow for some comparisons across gender, class, and ethnicity. Included here is an analysis of whether self-defined champions of various groups are more inclined than other MPs to be in personal contact with a cabinet minister on behalf of the specific group. Figure 7.3 includes three diagrams. The first diagram shows the percentage who have been in contact with a minister on behalf of women among self-defined champions of women's interests compared with other MPs. The second diagram shows the percentage who have been in contact with a minister on behalf of workers among self-defined champions of workers' interests compared with other MPs. The third diagram shows the percentage who have been in contact with a minister on behalf of immigrants among self-defined champions of immigrants' interests compared with other MPs.

The results in Figure 7.3 indicate that the effect of being a self-defined champion is most evident when it comes to immigrants' interests: 51 percent among self-defined champions have been in contact with a minister on behalf of this group compared with 22 percent among other MPs (a difference of 29 percentage points). When it comes to women's interests, the corresponding figures are 35 percent among self-defined champions and 16 percent among other MPs (a difference of 19 percentage points); and finally, when it comes to workers' interests, the corresponding figures are 39 percent among self-defined champions and 31 percent among other MPs (a difference of 8 percentage points). Thus, the main result, that group awareness matters, holds across multiple categories (cf. Esaiasson 2000).

The analysis presented above relies on one single indicator, but additional analysis of attitudes toward different concrete policy proposals supports the finding that being a self-defined champion of immigrants' interests has a significant effect: Self-defined champions of immigrants' interests are more supportive than others toward proposals such as "increase financial support for immigrants so they can preserve their own culture," and "immigrants in Sweden should be able to practice their religion freely here," and less supportive of proposals such as "accept fewer refugees into Sweden," and "reduce Swedish aid to developing nations." At the same time, being a self-defined champion is linked to MPs' personal background characteristics (Wängnerud 2012). The theory on the politics of awareness cannot simply replace the theory on the politics of presence.

Comparisons with other countries

Sweden is a deviant case in the global community; however, one needs to think carefully about the aspects that may matter for the analysis presented in this book. One such factor is party competition, since the risk of experiencing significant losses makes political parties more inclined to promote gender equality. In Sweden this was particularly evident at the beginning of

The politics of feminist awareness 141

Percentage answering that they at least once during the last year have been in personal contact with a Minister on behalf of the different groups

a) Self-defined champions of women's interests 2010

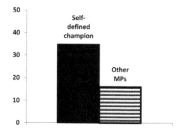

b) Self-defined champions of worker's interests 2010

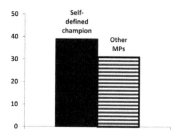

c) Self-defined champions of immigrant's interests 2010

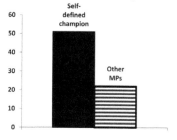

Figure 7.3 Acting in the interests of women, workers and immigrants
The question reads: "During the past year, how often have you personally contacted cabinet ministers to put forward preferences of women/women's organizations, worker/work organizations, refugees/immigrants organizations?" The response alternatives were: "at least once a month," "sometimes," and "never." Included here is the percentage answering "at least once a month" or "sometimes." Self-defined champion is based on the question: "How important do you personally find the following tasks to be?" Included are responses to "Promoting the interests/views of workers," "Promoting the interests/views of women," and "Promoting the interests/views of refugees/immigrants." A self-defined champion assesses the task to be "very important."
(Swedish Parliamentary Survey, Department of Political Science, University of Gothenburg, 2010)

the 1970s, when Gunnar Helén, the former leader of the Liberal Party, and Olof Palme, the former leader of the Social Democratic Party, started a competition to be the most women-friendly, and in the election of 1994, when the feminist network the Support Stockings put pressure on all established parties. Countries with low party competition may lack the extra spark needed to set such developments in motion.

Another prominent feature may be the one-dimensionality of the Swedish party system. In recent decades Sweden has experienced the entrance into the Riksdag of a Christian Democratic Party and a Green Party, and also two different right-wing populist parties, New Democracy and the Sweden Democrats. However the left–right dimension is, in all respects, considered strong. The lack of strong conflicts based on, for example, religion or region, visible in many other European countries, may be an enabling factor for the gender dimension to grow in importance.

Epilogue: Was the 2014 election the end of Swedish exceptionalism?

A general election was held in Sweden in September 2014. After two terms, 2006–10 and 2010–14, with the Alliance coalition in government, Sweden is now governed by a coalition of the Social Democratic Party and the Green Party. The new government has declared that one of their priorities is to be a "feminist" government. The cabinet is made up of 12 women and 12 men. More interesting to note, perhaps, is that women hold portfolios such as foreign affairs, finance, and the labor market. To have women in all these highly ranked portfolios at the same time is unusual.

In the 2014 election the Feminist Initiative, a political party founded in 2005, played an important role. In the election to the European Parliament in May 2014 the Feminist Initiative gained 5.3 percent of the vote, which meant that they were entitled to representation (one representative). In the election to the Riksdag support for the party turned out to be lower, at 3.1 percent; this is below the threshold of 4 percent needed to be represented in the parliament. However, in that same election the Feminist Initiative gained seats in 13 local councils in Sweden. Future studies will probably show that the activities of the Feminist Initiative contributed to increased attention for feminism and gender equality in the 2014 election campaign. However, in contrast to the 1994 election when the feminist network the Support Stockings was active, the events in 2014 probably had a more restricted effect – that is, only reaching the left-green parties.

Preliminary analyses in the form of, exit polls conducted by Swedish Television, show that the Feminist Initiative mainly took votes from the Green Party, the Left Party, and the Social Democratic Party. Against the backdrop of strategic reasoning, it comes as no surprise that the new government put emphasis on feminism and gender equality. There is a risk of realizing significant additional losses in subsequent elections. One forecast is that the new government, to be trustworthy and competitive, will produce policies that strengthen the position of women vis-à-vis men. However, also in the 2014 Swedish election the right-wing populist party the Sweden Democrats became the third biggest party in the Riksdag, with almost 13 percent of the vote, and is currently in a so-called swing vote position. The governing coalition between the Social Democratic Party and the Green Party is one of the weakest governing minority coalitions Sweden has experienced. New forms of informal coalitions have to emerge. The more pessimistic forecast is that the breakthrough for feminism in the 2014 election will be a "hollow prize" leading to few changes (cf. Kraus and Swanstrom 2001). Prominent political scientists have already declared that the election of 2014 means the end of Swedish exceptionalism (Rothstein 2014).

Bibliography

Ahlbäck Öberg, Shirin, Jörgen Hermansson and Lena Wängnerud. 2007. *Exit riksdagen*. Malmö: Liber.
Bergqvist, Christina, Anette Borchost, Ann-Dorte Christensen, Viveca Ramstedt-Silén, Nina C. Rauum and Auður Styrkársdóttir. 2000. *Equal Democracies? Gender and Politics in the Nordic Countries*. Oslo: Norwegian University Press.
Bolzendahl, Catherine. 2014. "Opportunities and Expectations: The Gendered Organization of Legislative Committees in Germany, Sweden, and the United States." *Gender & Society*, published online August 1, 2014.
Bolzendahl, Catherine I. and Daniel J. Myers. 2004. "Feminist Attitudes and Support for Gender Equality: Opinion Change in Women and Men, 1974–1998." *Social Forces* 83: 759–789.
Dahlerup, Drude and Monique Leyenaar, eds. 2013. *Breaking Male Dominance in Old Democracies*. Oxford: Oxford University Press.
Esaiasson, Peter. 2000. "How Members of Parliament Define their Task." In *Beyond Westminster and Congress: The Nordic Experience*, ed. Peter Esaiasson and Knut Heidar. Columbus: Ohio State University Press.
Haavio-Mannila, Elina et al. 1983. *Det uferdige demokartiet. Kvinner i nordisk politikk*. Oslo: Nordisk ministerråd. (Published in English as *Unfinished Democracy: Women in Nordic Politics*. Oxford: Pergamon Press, 1985.)
Htun, Mala and Laurel S. Weldon. 2012. "The Civic Origins of Progressive Policy Change: Combating Violence Against Women in Global Perspective, 1975–2005." *American Political Science Review* 106(3): 548–569.
Inglehart, Ronald and Pippa Norris. 2003. *Rising Tide: Gender Equality and Cultural Change Around the World*. Cambridge: Cambridge University Press.
Kraus, Neil and Todd Swanstrom. 2001. "Minority Mayors and the Hollow-prize Problem." *Political Science and Politics* 34(1): 99–105.
Phillips, Anne. 2007. *Multiculturalism Without Culture*. Princeton, NJ: Princeton University Press.
Pitkin, Hanna F.. 1967. *The Concept of Representation*. Berkeley: University of California Press.
Rothstein, Bo. 2014. "The End of Swedish Exceptionalism." *Foreign Affairs* 18 September.
Skjeie, Hege. 1992. *Den politiske betydningen av kjønn. En studie av norsk topp-politikk*. Rapport 92.11. PhD diss., Oslo: Institutt for Samfunnsforskning.

Squires, Judith. 1999. *Gender and Political Theory*. Cambridge: Polity Press.
Verloo, Mieke. 2005. "Displacement and Empowerment: Reflections on the Concept and Practice of the Council of Europe Approach to Gender Mainstreaming and Gender Equality." *Social Politics* 12(3): 344–365.
Wängnerud, Lena. 1998. *Politikens andra sida. Om kvinnorepresentation i Sveriges Riksdag*. PhD diss., University of Gothenburg.
Wängnerud, Lena. 2000. "Testing the Politics of Presence: Women's Representation in the Swedish Riksdag." *Scandinavian Political Studies* 23(1): 67–91.
Wängnerud, Lena. 2012. "Testing the Politics of Presence: A Comparative Study on the Importance of Gender, Class, and Ethnicity in the Swedish Parliament." Paper presented at the internal conference on Multidisciplinary Opinion and Democracy, Department of Political Science, University of Gothenburg, 13 October.
Yoo, Eunhye. 2012. "The Impact of Domestic and Transnational Conditions." *Politics & Gender* 8: 304–340.

Appendix I
A note on the methodology

In this book Sweden is used as a critical case for studying the complex relationship between the descriptive and substantive representation of women. Sweden is interesting because the number of women elected to the national parliament has been high for quite some time. Currently, women hold 44 percent of the seats in the Riksdag, Sweden's parliament; the average for national parliaments in Europe is 25.3 percent (www.ipu.org).

Another reason for studying Sweden is that it is a country for which there exists an impressive amount of data. The data in this book are mainly drawn from three sets of sources:

i *Statistics Sweden*, which is a government agency. The statistics produced are used as a basis for decision making, but also for debates and research. Statistics Sweden has a coordination role for the official statistics of Sweden. It produces the report *Women and Men in Sweden: Facts and Figures*, which is updated regularly. The report is available through the website (www.scb.se).
ii *The Riksdag*, the national parliament. Most important for this book are the Parliamentary Members rolls produced on a yearly basis. These rolls list members in each standing committee but also in other positions linked to the role as an MP. There is turnover in the Riksdag between elections and an MP leaving the Riksdag is substituted by the person next to him/her on the party list. Once the speaker and the three vice-speakers are elected, they are substituted, which is also the case for cabinet ministers who are recruited from the Riksdag. For example, this means that the number of women in the Riksdag may vary from the start to the end of a parliamentary term. When calculating the proportion of women in the standing committees, changes that occur between elections are especially important to take into account. The calculations in Table 4.1 build on averages for each committee for each year during a political term.
iii *The Swedish Parliamentary Surveys*, conducted by scholars at the Department of Political Science, University of Gothenburg. This is a

unique series of surveys which will be explained in more detail below. Principal investigators for the surveys used in this book have been: 1985 and 1988 Peter Esaiasson and Sören Holmberg; 1994 Martin Brothén, Peter Esaiasson and Sören Holmberg; 1998, 2002, and 2006 Martin Brothén and Sören Holmberg; 2010 Peter Esaiasson, Mikael Gilljam, Sören Holmberg and Lena Wängnerud. The main results of the studies have been published in a series of books and numerous scholarly articles, one of the most important publications being *Representation from Above. Members of Parliament and Representative Democracy in Sweden*, by Peter Esaiasson and Sören Holmberg (Aldershot: Dartmouth Publishing, 1996).

The Swedish Parliamentary Surveys

The main purpose of The Swedish Parliamentary Surveys is to study the parliamentary role in representative democracy based on the general election. More specifically, it aims to secure opportunities for future social science research on the basis of a series of surveys consisting of questionnaires with all members of the Riksdag. The questions included are coordinated with questions to voters included in surveys from the Swedish National Elections Study (SNES) Program, which is also based at the Department of Political Science, University of Gothenburg. The exact questions included in the parliamentary surveys vary between survey occasions, depending on the interests of principal investigators, but themes covered are typically activities during the election campaign; ideological standpoints and attitudes toward the political system; political priorities and attitudes toward concrete policy proposals; assessments of internal parliamentary work; and background characteristics.

The Swedish Parliamentary Surveys are typically send out to MPs in November of an election year (elections are held in September). The field work goes on for about six months. Response rates are high: 97 percent in 1985, 96 percent in 1988, 97 percent in 1994, 94 percent in 1998, 94 percent in 2002, 94 percent in 2006, and 89 percent in 2010. Note that there was no survey after the election in 1991. The surveys have been funded by the University of Gothenburg and the Swedish Foundation for Humanities and Social Sciences.

Since almost all MPs participate, the data generated through the Swedish Parliamentary Surveys can be handled as covering a total population. In this book, however, a significance level of 0.10 is used as a rule of thumb; differences below that level are usually not commented on. Instead of reporting the number of respondents in connection to each figure or table, I provide a list of respondents for each party (women/men) on each survey occasion:

The analysis in the book builds on more analyses than reported in tables and figures. The criteria for reporting results in a table/figure is that the

Table A.1 Number of survey respondents (women/men)

	1985	1988	1994	1998	2002	2006	2010
Left Party	3/16	8/11	10/11	17/25	14/15	14/7	10/8
Social Democratic Party	55/103	63/90	77/82	61/60	62/72	60/61	50/56
Green Party	–	8/11	10/8	7/8	8/5	9/9	13/9
Center Party	13/29	16/26	10/17	10/8	10/11	10/17	5/14
Liberal Party	19/30	17/25	9/17	7/8	23/23	13/12	9/12
Conservative Party	16/56	16/45	19/52	24/53	21/30	37/54	42/49
Christian Democratic Party	–	–	5/10	15/24	10/23	11/13	7/10
Sweden Democrats	–	–	–	–	–	–	2/14
Total	106/234	128/208	140/197	141/186	148/179	154/173	138/172

most important results should be included in the book, but an additional criterion is that the results reported should be relatively easy to follow. The notes included below the tables/figures explain the most important choices in each analysis. Below follows additional description on some of the core analyses.

Description of variables

Dependent variables

Table 2.2 Determinants of attitudes among Swedish MPs toward two arguments for an equal distribution of women and men in parliament. The question reads: "There may be various reasons for advocating an even distribution between women and men in parliament. How important do you consider the following reasons: The composition should reflect the most important groups in society; there will be consequences on policies." The following response alternatives were offered: "very important," "fairly important," "not very important," and "not at all important."

1 "fairly important", "not very important", "not at all important"
2 "very important"

Table 3.2 Determinants of Swedish MPs' commitment to represent women's interests and concerns. The question reads "How important are the following tasks to you personally as a member of parliament? Promote the interest/views of women." The MPs were asked to rank about ten representative tasks. The following response alternatives were offered: "very important," "fairly important," "not very important," and "not at all important."

1 "fairly important," "not very important," "not at all important"
2 "very important"

Table 4.4 Determinants of Swedish MPs' assessments of party group working conditions. The question reads: "Generally speaking, what do you think of your personal working conditions in parliament, the Riksdag's working conditions, and your own group's working conditions: Party group working conditions." The following response alternatives were offered: "good as it is," "mostly good as it is," "needs improvement in several areas," and "needs fundamental change."

1 "needs improvement in several areas," "needs fundamental change"
2 "good as it is," "mostly good as it is"

Table 4.6 Determinants of Swedish MPs' assessment of their ability to impact their own party groups' positions. The question reads: "How do you rate your ability to impact your party group's positions on various issues: Issues within my own area of expertise." The MPs were also asked to rank their ability to impact their party group's position on issues outside their own area of expertise. The following response alternatives were offered: "very good," "fairly good," "fairly bad," and "very bad."

1 "fairly good," "fairly bad," "very bad"
2 "very good"

Table 5.3 Determinants of Swedish MPs' priorities for welfare politics as an area of personal interest. The question reads: "Which area or areas in politics are you most interested in?" The question is open ended and respondents were permitted to choose any area or areas. Up to three areas were coded.

1 the respondent has not answered anything related to the policy areas; social policy, family policy, senior citizens/care of elderly or health care
2 the respondent has answered social policy, family policy, senior citizens/care of elderly, health care or similar answers

Independent variables

The focus of the study is on the sex/gender category. However, throughout the book a number of other independent variables are included. The selection is based on previous research and included are a set of standard variables in research on political representation and research on parliaments as institutions. Besides gender (which is coded 0 "men," 1 "women"), party affiliation is the most important category. The Conservative Party is used as a reference category for the parties in all regression analyses. The other independent variables are coded as follows:

Age. Age of the respondent in years.
Experience. How many years the respondent has been a member of the parliament.
Education. The highest level of education attained by the respondent. 0 "lower education," 1 "higher education" (higher studies at college/university, graduated from college/university, graduate).
Power position. 0 "no power position," 1 "power position" (holders of a power position are MPs who are members of: the party's council of trust, the party executive/party board, or are the leader of the parliament's party group, chair or vice-chair of the parliament's standing committees).

Appendix II
A note on Swedish politics

For those with a particular interest in Swedish politics, there follows a description of the Swedish political system. Information in English is available on the websites www.riksdagen.se and www.regeringen.se. In all cases except one I have followed official English translations for the names of the Swedish parties. In this book I use the label "The Conservative Party," whereas the official translation would be "The Moderate Party."

Elections

In Sweden general elections are held every four years, with the last election being held on September 14, 2014. Around 7 million people are entitled to vote and thereby influence which political party will represent them in the Riksdag (the Swedish Parliament), county councils and municipalities. Elections to all levels of government are held on the same day.

The 349-member Riksdag is Sweden's primary representative forum. The entire Riksdag is chosen by direct elections based on suffrage for all Swedish citizens aged 18 or over who are, or previously have been, residents of Sweden. Since 1971 Sweden has had a unicameral (one-chamber) Riksdag. Eligibility to serve in the Riksdag requires Swedish citizenship and the attainment of voting age. Candidates must be nominated by a political party. All elections employ the principle of proportional representation, to ensure that seats are distributed among the political parties in proportion to the votes cast for them across the country as a whole. There is one exception to the rule of full national proportionality: a party must receive at least 4 percent of the vote in the election to gain representation in the Riksdag, a rule designed to prevent very small parties from getting in.

Distribution of seats in the Riksdag

In elections to the Riksdag Sweden is divided into 29 constituencies. The 349 seats consist of 310 fixed constituency seats and 39 filled by adjustment. The number of fixed constituency seats in each constituency is based on the number of people who are entitled to vote in the constituency. The distribution of these seats reflects the election results in each constituency.

The election authority allocates the fixed seats between the parties according to a method known as the adjusted odd numbers method. In broad terms, the number of votes for each party is divided by a series of numbers until the 310 seats have been distributed.

The purpose of the 39 adjustment seats is to achieve the best possible proportional distribution of seats between the parties for the country as a whole. First, the country is regarded as a single constituency and this is then compared with the distribution of seats in the various constituencies. The adjustment seats are first allocated according to party and then according to constituency. In the current Riksdag the number of seats distributed to constituencies varies from two (Gotlands län) to 32 (Stockholms kommun).

The personal vote

The final stage involves the distribution of seats among the parties' candidates. If 5 percent of those who have voted for a particular party in a constituency have cast a vote for the same candidate, that candidate obtains a seat in the Riksdag. If several candidates have fulfilled this requirement, the seats are allocated on the basis of the number of personalized votes. The personal vote was introduced in Sweden in 1998.

The cabinet

Formally, the Riksdag makes the decisions and the government implements them. The government also submits proposals for new laws or law amendments to the Riksdag.

The government governs the country but is accountable to the Riksdag. The Riksdag appoints a prime minister, who is tasked with forming a government. The prime minister personally chooses the ministers to make up the cabinet and also decides which ministers will be in charge of the various ministries. Together, the prime minister and the cabinet ministers form the government. Under the constitution, the government – not the head of state (the monarch) – is empowered to make governmental decisions. Ministers usually represent the political party or parties in power. In many cases they have a seat in the Riksdag, which they retain during their time in the cabinet, although an alternate takes over the duties of a Riksdag member appointed to the cabinet. In other words, a cabinet minister must abstain from voting in the Riksdag. All ministers are, however, entitled to participate in parliamentary debates.

At the official opening of the Riksdag each September, the prime minister delivers a statement of government policy. In it the prime minister presents the government's policy goals for the coming year and defines priority policy areas at the national and international levels. The government rules Sweden by implementing the decisions of the Riksdag and by formulating new laws or law amendments, on which the Riksdag decides. The government is assisted in this task by the government offices and some 360 government agencies. The cabinet as a whole is responsible for all government decisions. Although many routine matters are in practice decided by individual ministers and only formally approved by the government, the principle of collective responsibility is reflected in all governmental work.

History of Swedish elections

Sweden's general elections in September 2014 resulted in a minority coalition of Social Democrats and Greens taking over after the center-right Alliance coalition. For many decades, the Social Democratic Party had a dominant role in Swedish politics. However, over the past 30 years or so, power has changed hands several times between the Social Democrats and the "non-socialist" political bloc.

Following the 2014 general election, Stefan Löfven became prime minister, although his coalition of Social Democrats and Greens could not gain an absolute majority. The prime minister's Social Democratic Party garnered 31 percent of the vote. Together with the Green Party's 6.9 percent, the left-of-centre coalition thereby achieved 37.9 percent. The center-right Alliance, which includes the Conservative Party, the Liberal Party, the Center Party and the Christian Democrats, collected 39.4 percent of the vote. Since Sweden has a system of negative parliamentarism, meaning that a government can stay in power as long as it does not have a majority against it, the Social Democrats and the Greens could still form a government by themselves.

In short, the 2014 elections left Sweden in a comparatively complicated parliamentary situation. A left-of-centre minority coalition is in government and the far-right Sweden Democrats are in a so-called swing vote position, having gained nearly 13 percent of the vote.

The 2014 election in light of previous elections

1932–1976	The Social Democrats rule without interruption, except for a period of 109 days in 1936 when Sweden has an interim government.
1976	The Social Democrats are defeated by a coalition consisting of the Center Party, the Conservative Party, and the Liberal Party.
1979	The non-socialist parties retain their parliamentary majority, and a new three-party government is formed. In the spring of 1981, the Conservative Party leaves the government.
1982	The non-socialist parties lose their majority and a Social Democratic minority government is formed.

1985 and 1988 The Social Democrats remain in power after both elections.
1991 A non-socialist minority government of the Conservative Party, the Liberal Party, the Center Party, and the Christian Democratic Party is formed.
1994 The Social Democrats form a minority government.
1998 and 2002 The Social Democrats remain in office after both elections, but in order to implement their policies are forced to form a parliamentary alliance with the Left Party and the Green Party.
2006 The non-socialist parties form a four-party majority coalition government called the Alliance.
2010 The ruling center-right Alliance stays in power, but fails to gain an outright majority.
2014 A minority left-of-centre coalition takes over after the Alliance.

Gender gaps in party choice in Sweden

The Swedish National Elections Study (SNES) Program started in 1956. SNES provides information on gender gaps in party choice in Sweden. Table A2a and Table A2b include results for parties that have won a seat in the Riksdag. There are no results yet for the 2014 election.

Table A.2a The gender gap in party choice in Sweden, 1956–2010

Year	Left Party % Wom	Men	diff.	Social Democratic Party % Wom	Men	diff.	Green Party % Wom	Men	diff.	New Democracy % Wom	Men	diff.	Sweden Democrats % Wom	Men	diff.
1956	1	2	-1	48	49	-1	–	–	–	–	–	–	–	–	–
1960	1	3	-2	53	51	-2	–	–	–	–	–	–	–	–	–
1964	2	3	-1	50	53	-3	–	–	–	–	–	–	–	–	–
1968	1	2	-1	54	54	0	–	–	–	–	–	–	–	–	–
1970	3	6	-3	48	48	0	–	–	–	–	–	–	–	–	–
1973	3	5	-2	47	46	+1	–	–	–	–	–	–	–	–	–
1976	4	4	0	45	46	-1	–	–	–	–	–	–	–	–	–
1979	5	6	-1	45	44	+1	–	–	–	–	–	–	–	–	–
1982	4	6	-2	48	46	+2	2	1	+1	–	–	–	–	–	–
1985	5	6	-1	46	41	+5	2	2	0	–	–	–	–	–	–
1988	6	5	+1	47	43	+4	6	6	0	–	–	–	–	–	–
1991	4	4	0	37	37	0	5	2	+3	6	9	-3	–	–	–
1994	8	6	+2	45	47	-2	6	4	+2	0	1	-1	–	–	–
1998	14	9	+5	35	40	-5	5	4	+1	–	–	–	–	–	–
2002	10	7	+3	38	40	-2	7	6	+1	–	–	–	–	–	–
2006	6	5	+1	35	36	-1	8	4	+4	–	–	–	1	3	-2
2010	5	6	-1	33	29	+4	10	8	+2	–	–	–	2	5	-3

Table A.2b The gender gap in party choice in Sweden, 1956–2010

Year	Center Party % Wom	Men	diff.	Liberal Party % Wom	Men	diff.	Christian Democratic Party % Wom	Men	diff.	Conservative Party % Wom	Men	diff.
1956	8	10	-2	27	25	-2	–	–		16	14	+2
1960	15	16	+1	17	16	+1	–	–		14	14	0
1964	13	17	-4	18	15	+3	2	2	0	13	9	+4
1968	16	19	-3	15	13	+2	2	2	0	12	10	+2
1970	24	24	0	15	12	+3	2	1	+1	8	8	0
1973	26	26	0	9	8	+1	2	2	0	13	13	0
1976	24	22	+2	12	12	0	2	1	+1	13	14	-1
1979	19	15	+4	11	11	0	2	1	+1	18	22	-4
1982	15	15	0	7	5	+2	3	2	+1	21	25	-4
1985	10	11	-1	18	15	+3	3	2	+1	16	23	-7
1988	11	12	-1	12	12	0	4	2	+2	14	19	-5
1991	10	8	+2	10	8	+2	8	7	+1	19	24	-5
1994	10	7	+3	9	7	+2	5	4	+1	17	24	-7
1998	5	5	0	6	4	+2	13	9	+4	20	27	-7
2002	6	6	0	16	16	0	10	8	+2	12	15	-3
2006	8	8	0	7	8	+1	8	6	+2	25	28	-3
2010	9	4	+5	8	7	+1	5	5	0	27	35	-8

(Tables adapted from Henrik Oscarsson and Sören Holmberg. 2008. Regeringsskifte. Väljarna och valet 2006. Stockholm: Norstedts Juridik, p.332; and Henrik Oscarsson and Sören Holmberg. 2013. Nya svenska väljare. Stockholm: Norstedts Juridik, 80)

Index

accountability 10–11
actual assignment 64
Alliance parties 33, 133, 143
area of: expertise 73, 79; personal interest 85–7, 90–3, 98, 138; responsibility 7, 63, 78
autonomy 39, 155

balance of power 41, 55, 84–7, 139
basic functions committees 64–6
Beckwith Karen 99
board chair 59, 62–3
Bolzendahl Catherine 47, 78, 136
Bratton Kathleen A. 114, 116
Brothén Martin 147

cabinet minister 59, 62, 66–8
capability approach 38–9, 54, 105
case studies 113–4
care-and-career politics 41
Celis Karen 4, 88
center-right parties/bloc 22, 25–9, 33, 69, 100, 118
Center Party 25–9, 62, 77, 132
Childs Sarah 4, 88
child-bearing 4, 38
childcare coverage 38, 94, 114, 116
Christian Democratic Party 23–9, 143
civil rights 38, 48, 94
citizen's everyday lives 2, 4, 11, 43, 104–5, 114–16
claim-making 10
class 14–15, 139, 141
coercion 60
contextual approach 10, 13, 37–9, 55, 79, 101, 104, 139
cohort effects 48
commitment to gender equality 18–19, 26–7, 72, 137
commitment: strength 33, 134; type 134
committee assignments 60–6, 92, 137

conflict work-family 40–5, 56, 84, 88, 94
conflicting interests 13–14
Conservative Party 19–20, 25–9, 76, 82, 132–3
constituencies 11, 151–2
contagion effects 20, 23
critical: acts 7, 110; mass 6–7, 110, 127
cross-sectional analysis 100
cultural change 115, 123
culture/law committees 64–6

daddy month 113, 121
Dahl Birgitta 59
Dahlerup Drude 9, 18, 26, 37, 47, 61, 136
descriptive representation 4–5, 12, 19, 33, 47, 105, 114, 122, 139
disadvantaged group 8, 96, 110
discourse on difference 26
Dodson Deborah 5
dominant norms 32
dual breadwinner model 39
dynamic explanatory themes 47

economic development 3, 104–5
economic independence 9, 40, 108, 124
economy/technology committees 64–6, 78–9, 137
egalitarian: societies 26; trending 61, 136; values 115, 117, 123
eight-party system 23
elected: assemblies 60–1, 118, 121, 139; representatives 10, 18–19, 26–7, 56, 59, 79, 84, 89, 127, 132
elitism 36, 41
employment: full-time 100, 115, 117, 121; part-time 40, 117–18, 127
endogenous factors 2, 36
Esaiasson Peter 147
ethnicity 14–15, 36, 139, 141

equal opportunities 111–12
equality policies targeting men 106, 113, 127, 140
equality policies targeting women 19, 106, 114, 127, 140
equality processes 104–5, 112, 117, 121, 123, 132
exogenous factors 2, 13, 23
exposure-based approaches 47, 49, 133

family policy 7, 90, 104–5
femininity 78, 89, 112, 136–7
feminism/feminist ideals 10, 18, 23, 47, 126, 133–4, 144
Feminist Initiative 62, 143
feminist institutionalism 26, 48–9, 60–1, 78
feminist mobilization 8
feminists: strong 97–8; weak 97–8
fervent champions/representatives 48, 50, 121
Firestone Juanita M. 89
five-party system 23, 25
formal political institutions 7–11, 14
formal power 60, 62, 66
functional divisions/gender structures 7, 14, 59–60, 79, 136

gender balance 9, 21, 61
gender discrimination 85, 138
gender equal democracies 39, 84, 138
gender mainstreaming 106, 127, 140
gender neutral 61, 78, 106, 127
gender quota 21
gender: equality scale 123; equality standard 32
gender empowerment index 115
gender equity index 122, 124, 126, 135, 140
gendered institutions 61
gender-gap index 122, 124, 126, 135, 140
gender gap: in turnout 19, 41; in party choice 20, 82, 154
gender-related development index 115
gender related: norms 18, 26; differences 38–9, 41, 43, 84
gender-specific obstacles 5–6, 14, 78–9
general election 10, 11, 13, 87, 89
generational gap 75
Gilljam Mikael 147
global arena 104, 121–3, 140
Green Party 21, 23, 25–9, 100, 143–4
group awareness 8, 47, 54, 96, 124, 132–4, 140
Guadagnini Marika 10–11

health care 43, 45, 90, 94, 96, 100
Helén Gunnar 1, 19–20, 143
Hernes Helga 10
hierarchical gender structures 60, 136–7
Hirdman Yvonne 22–3
Holmberg Sören 147
horizontal sex segregation 60, 136
Htun Mala 8
Human rights dataset 124

ideas/strategies of inclusion 27, 33, 132–33
ideas/strategies of reversal 27, 31, 54, 132–33
ideological gender gap 82
ideological: position 18, 26; shifts 18, 25–6, 132
individual level of analysis 59
individualization 108–9
informal power/norms 14, 26–7, 48, 59, 64, 66–7, 72
Inglehart Ronald 115, 117, 123
institutional level of analysis 59
institutionalized gender equality 27
intentional 8, 12–13, 47, 96
interest-based approaches 47
internal working procedures 6–9, 33, 59, 100, 135–7
internal party documents 13, 20
intersectionality 139

Jeydal Alana 89
Jónasdóttir Anna G. 54
justice for women 20, 94

Kantola Johanna 88
Kittilson Miki Caul 37
Krook Mona Lena 88

labor force surveys 127
left-green parties/bloc 23, 26–9, 33, 59, 72, 100, 118, 121, 133, 143
Left Party 20–6, 59, 100, 143
left-right dimension 29, 33, 53, 100, 133, 143
legislative behavior 12, 37, 89
level of democracy 105, 124, 126
Leyenaar Monique 9, 18, 37, 136
liberal democracy 14
Liberal Party 1, 19–29, 132–33, 143
linear process 2, 13, 23, 87, 135
local government/municipal councils 18, 75, 104, 114–17, 139, 143
longitudinal design 100
long-term perspective 77, 104, 106, 108, 140

Lovenduski, Joni 4, 10–11, 61
loyal party worker 77–8, 137

male breadwinner model 39
male dominance 9, 61
marginalization 37–8
marketization 84, 100
masculine dominance gendered organization 61
masculine 61, 78
Matland Richard 20
Mazur Amy G. 9–10, 87
McBride Dorothy E. 9–10, 87
Mill John Stuart 105
minister for gender equality 63, 106
model of gender parity 18
modernization 3, 115, 117, 122–4, 127, 140
multiple categories 14, 141

New Democracy 22–3, 26, 143
newcomer 49, 52–3, 59, 134
nonmilitary government expenditure 82–3
non-parliamentary women's organizations 5, 85, 113, 140
normative assessments 37, 41
Norris Pippa 115, 117, 123
Nussbaum Martha 105

official documents 18, 139–40
opinion-formation processes 47
opposition parties 69, 75
Osborn, Tracy 13, 18, 37–8, 41
outcomes in everyday lives of citizens 4, 13, 104, 114, 121–2, 126, 139

Palme, Olof 1, 19–20, 143
paid labor force 2, 40, 43, 127
parental allowance/leave 2, 88, 112–121, 139
parliamentary experience 28, 50
parliamentary laws/regulations 14, 26
parliamentary party group 23, 25, 59, 66, 72, 75
parliamentary process 11, 18–19, 40, 69, 89, 99, 113, 139–40
party: affiliation 28, 98, 117; delegations 82; membership 41; system 23, 25, 132, 143
party group's position 67, 72–3, 75, 104, 113
patriarchal parliament 6, 9
perceived impact/influence 62, 72–3
period-specific events 13, 48

personal integrity 40, 41, 43, 46, 56, 84, 94
Phillips Anne 3–4, 7, 12, 14, 33, 36, 38–9, 41, 83, 97, 114
Pitkin Hanna 7, 11, 37, 39, 89, 139
polarized gendered organization 61
policy change argument 29
policy networks 67
policy promotion 14, 83, 140
political agenda 1, 4, 6, 43, 47, 82–3, 94, 100, 105, 138
political attitudes 14, 27, 32, 43, 45, 48, 77, 83, 94–7,134
political inclusion 41, 43, 139
political institutions 3–9, 61
political landscape 25, 132
political priorities 12, 14, 43, 55, 60, 67, 90, 99, 121, 134, 140
political process 5–6, 11
political representation 7, 10–11, 14, 43, 67, 88–9
politics of awareness 8, 47, 54, 96–100, 126, 133
politics of presence 3–5, 11–12, 47, 54, 83, 96–8, 100, 134, 141
politicization 39, 84, 138
pornography 43–45, 94–100, 134, 138
power position 7, 14, 28, 59, 137
preexisting interests 88
preferences for committees 60–1, 64, 137
private sector 40
public sector 40, 43, 45, 82, 84, 94–100, 118

qualitative interviews 64, 66, 75–77, 137
Quality of Government Institute 12

radical feminism/feminists 23, 27, 31, 52
right-wing populist parties 22, 23, 26, 143–44
Ray Leonard P. 114, 116
recognition of women 8, 41, 55–6, 85, 139
recruitment of women 18, 36, 82
redistribution of resources 94
reflect argument 29, 31
Reingold Beth 37–8, 60
representative democracy 2, 6, 13, 19
reproductive rights/abortion 38, 106, 110
responsive/responsiveness 7, 11, 14, 37, 39, 89, 115
rhetoric on difference 88
Rosenbluth Frances 82–3
Rothstein Bo 128
RNGS, research network on gender, politics, and the state 9–10

Salmond Ron 83
Save the Children 2
Saward Michael 10, 88
Scandinavian/Swedish: welfare states 13, 39–42, 56, 84, 92, 100–1, 139; exceptionalism 82, 143
Schwindt-Bayer Leslie 37–8, 60, 114
self-authorization 9–10, 87
self-defined champion 37, 46, 49, 52–6, 88, 97, 99, 141
self-determination 13, 36–41, 54, 84, 89, 131
self-reflection 13, 21
Sen Amartya 105
Senior government ministry officials 67
Swedish Sex Purchase Act 113, 124
short-term perspective 123, 140
Sinclair Barbara 48
six-hour workday 43–6, 94–100, 134, 138
Skjeie Hege 41, 47, 88
social comparison theory 48
Social Democratic Party 1, 19–26, 84, 114, 143–44
social background 8, 12–13, 141
social group experiences 8, 47
social expenditures 83
social policy 43–6, 90–2, 104, 113
Social Watch 3, 104, 122, 124, 135, 140
social welfare committees 7, 64–6, 78–9, 137
soft quota 21
spill-over effect 47, 49–50, 56, 96
Squires Judith 27, 31
standing committee 7, 14, 28, 50, 59, 78–9, 92, 136–7
standstill 136, 138–9
state feminism 10
Statistics Sweden 40, 146
stereotyping 61, 78
strategic reasoning 20–1, 143
strategies/ideas of inclusion 27, 132–3
strategies/ideas of reversal 27, 132–3
Studlar Donley 20
subjective: left-right ideology 25; left-right dimension 29
subjective political interest 42
subjectively defined interests 88
subnational level 104, 114–16, 118, 121, 126, 140
substantive representation 4–5, 7, 12, 36, 46–7, 88, 105, 114, 117, 122, 139–40
substantive definition of women's interests 37
Support Stockings 22–3, 49, 66, 134, 137, 143

Svallfors Stefan 84
SNES, Swedish National Election Studies Program 12, 37, 41, 45, 55, 147
Swedish Crime Survey 40
Sweden Democrats 23, 26, 143–44
Swedish Parliamentary Survey 12, 19, 25, 27, 31, 66–7, 78, 83, 99, 141, 147
swing vote position 144, 153

Taylor Adrew J. 89
Thies Michael 82
Thomas Sue 60
traditional feminine sphere 113, 127
threshold numbers 6–7, 83,110
transformations of Swedish society 14, 104, 122, 127
transformative processes 27, 54, 121

United Nations 38–9, 105, 115, 122
unpaid care and household work 4, 38, 106
urbanization 117

Vega Arturo 89
Verloo Mieke 127, 140
violence against women 4, 8, 38, 40, 88, 94, 104, 106, 113
voting behavior/turnout 8, 19, 41, 43, 89

women as workers 94, 110, 140
Waylen Georgina 105–6
Weldon Laurel 8–9
welfare: politics 90–7, 100, 134, 138; state 14, 22, 37, 39–45, 82, 84, 92, 100–1, 139
western democracies 7, 89, 105
women-friendly policies 7–8, 10, 37, 83, 115, 132
women's interests 3, 36, 82, 133
women's: movement 9, 10, 87; organizations 5, 8, 85, 99, 113, 134, 138, 140
women's policy machinery 10–11
women's rights 8, 10, 14, 124, 126, 138
women's representation 1, 20, 60–1, 104, 113, 121
working conditions 5, 59, 67, 69, 72–5, 78, 137
World Economic Forum 3, 104, 122, 124, 135, 140

Young Iris Marion 8, 14, 96
Yoo Eunhye 8–9, 124

eBooks
from Taylor & Francis
Helping you to choose the right eBooks for your Library

Add to your library's digital collection today with Taylor & Francis eBooks. We have over 50,000 eBooks in the Humanities, Social Sciences, Behavioural Sciences, Built Environment and Law, from leading imprints, including Routledge, Focal Press and Psychology Press.

Choose from a range of subject packages or create your own!

Benefits for you
- Free MARC records
- COUNTER-compliant usage statistics
- Flexible purchase and pricing options
- 70% approx of our eBooks are now DRM-free.

Benefits for your user
- Off-site, anytime access via Athens or referring URL
- Print or copy pages or chapters
- Full content search
- Bookmark, highlight and annotate text
- Access to thousands of pages of quality research at the click of a button.

ORDER YOUR FREE INSTITUTIONAL TRIAL TODAY

Free Trials Available

We offer free trials to qualifying academic, corporate and government customers.

eCollections
Choose from 20 different subject eCollections, including:

- Asian Studies
- Economics
- Health Studies
- Law
- Middle East Studies

eFocus
We have 16 cutting-edge interdisciplinary collections, including:

- Development Studies
- The Environment
- Islam
- Korea
- Urban Studies

For more information, pricing enquiries or to order a free trial, please contact your local sales team:

UK/Rest of World: online.sales@tandf.co.uk
USA/Canada/Latin America: e-reference@taylorandfrancis.com
East/Southeast Asia: martin.jack@tandf.com.sg
India: journalsales@tandfindia.com

www.tandfebooks.com

#0195 - 311016 - C0 - 229/152/10 [12] - CB - 9781138802650